JUDAH AMONG THE EMPIRES

JUDAH AMONG THE EMPIRES

God's Purposes in Nahum, Habakkuk, and Zephaniah

Daniel C. Timmer

Reformation Heritage Books
Grand Rapids, Michigan

Reformation Heritage Books
3070 29th St. SE
Grand Rapids, MI 49512
616–977–0889
orders@heritagebooks.org
www.heritagebooks.org

Printed in the United States of America
23 24 25 26 27 28/10 9 8 7 6 5 4 3 2 1

Library of Congress Cataloging-in-Publication Data

Names: Timmer, Daniel C., author.
Title: Judah among the empires : God's purposes in Nahum, Habakkuk, and
    Zephaniah / Daniel C. Timmer.
Description: Grand Rapids, Michigan : Reformation Heritage Books, [2023] |
    Includes bibliographical references.
Identifiers: LCCN 2022045802 (print) | LCCN 2022045803 (ebook) |
    ISBN 9781601789907 (paperback) | ISBN 9781601789914 (epub)
Subjects: LCSH: Bible. Nahum—Commentaries. | Bible. Habakkuk—
    Commentaries. | Bible. Zephaniah—Commentaries.
Classification: LCC BS1625.53 .T558 2023 (print) | LCC BS1625.53
    (ebook) | DDC 224/.907—dc23/eng/20221202
LC record available at https://lccn.loc.gov/2022045802
LC ebook record available at https://lccn.loc.gov/2022045803

For additional Reformed literature, request a free book list from Reformation Heritage Books at the above regular or email address.

Contents

Preface

The Minor Prophets are, sadly, not very popular. This is certainly not due to any weakness or flaw in these inspired books. They are not the easiest type of literature to read, however, nor are they the most accessible because of their historical distance from us. This book was written in the hope that the Minor Prophets would not only become better known but would contribute to the theological, experiential, and practical enrichment and growth of God's people. To that end, the exposition of each prophetic book is preceded by a discussion of its historical context, shedding light on the theological issues that each prophetic book deals with. Reflection questions and a short list of recommended literature that further develops one or more points from the exposition are intended to help the reader engage the theological content of these books in a Christocentric way that integrates the prophets' message with the gospel and the Christian life.

Writing this book follows my teaching the Minor Prophets to seminary students for several years, most recently at the Evangelische Theologische Faculteit in Leuven, Belgium; and at Puritan Reformed Theological Seminary, Grand Rapids, Michigan. This book was written as I was completing a volume on Nahum, Habakkuk, and Zephaniah for Cambridge University Press, and despite their very different orientations and intended audiences, the two projects enriched each other. Their occasional overlap is indicated in several footnotes.

This book could not have been written without help and support from several people. First, I am grateful to Puritan Reformed Theological Seminary for its support of academic work that serves both the church and the academy. I am also thankful to the many students whose questions and insights have deepened my understanding of the Minor Prophets over the last fifteen years. Without the kind invitation of Mr. David Woollin, CEO of Reformation Heritage Books, this project would not have come into being, and subsequently it has benefited from the editorial expertise of Mr. Jay Collier and Mrs. Annette Gysen. Special thanks are due to my wife, Andreea, whose generous spirit, firm faith in God, and loving service to others are a model for me. Above all, I thank the triune God for His mercy and grace to me in Jesus Christ and for His call to serve His church in theological education and writing. It is my prayer that every reader would know His rich blessing as they study His Word and put it into practice as an expression of their love and gratitude to Him.

Introduction to Biblical Prophets and Their Books

The prophetic books present God's relationship with His chosen people and, through them, with the nations in "real time" (the prophet's present) and in the future. As such, they are fundamentally covenantal books. The Sinai covenant and its moral and religious norms are often the point of departure for prophetic critiques of Israel and Judah. This negative focus reflects the lamentable realities that had become dominant by the eighth century BC, when the earliest writing prophets Hosea and Amos began their ministries. By its nature, the Sinai covenant can announce only blessing on those who are obedient or condemnation on those who are disobedient. Sin's increasing dominance in both the Northern and Southern Kingdoms (Israel and Judah, respectively) meant that any message on that basis would be largely condemnatory. This has led many people to refer to faithful prophets as covenant prosecutors.

Happily, however, other covenants also play prominent roles in the prophetic books, and the prophets are more than prosecutors. Especially prominent are the Davidic covenant, in which God promised to maintain David's line as the shepherds of His people, and the Abrahamic covenant, in which God commits to being the God of Abraham and his descendants with the intention of bringing blessing to the nations through them. Unlike the conditional Sinai covenant, which could be and was broken by the long-term infidelity of most of God's people in the Old Testament, the Davidic and Abrahamic covenants are unconditional, meaning that they cannot be broken. This does not mean, however, that their blessings are guaranteed to all members of those covenants. Rather, while some external blessings, such as life in the Promised Land, were enjoyed by those without faith, the blessings that Abraham himself anticipated and ultimately enjoyed only after his death are granted to those who put their trust in God's promise to save His people through the Seed of the woman. Likewise, not all Davidic kings were equally faithful, and the interruption of the monarchy and the end of the theocracy in 586 BC underlined the inadequacy of these imperfect men as shepherds of God's people.

What Are the Prophetic Books About?

The prophetic message is thus one of judgment and salvation. Judgment on the nations of Israel and Judah becomes inevitable due to their sustained covenant unfaithfulness. But this impasse is overcome by God's progressive fulfillment of His promises to save within the framework of the Abrahamic, Davidic, and new covenants (Jeremiah 31). The ideal Davidic king is righteous and brings God's righteousness to His people (Jer. 23:4–6). The very concept of the people of God is refined by the prophets as they distinguish between "sinners" and the righteous who "feared the LORD" in Israel (Amos 9:8–10; Mal. 3:13–18). This in turn demonstrates that membership in the people of God is not an issue of ethnicity but of submission to God (Amos 9:11–12; Mic. 7:16–20). In this way, the fulfillment of the Abrahamic promise sees non-Israelites "joined to the LORD" (Zech. 2:11) and worshiping Him wherever they are, "from the rising of the sun, even to its going down" (Mal. 1:11). This also expands the idea of the Promised Land to the whole world, as the "many nations" that are Abraham's spiritual descendants turn to the Lord (Gen. 17:5–6). As Paul Williamson has shown, "Canaan was simply the preliminary stage in the ultimate unfolding of God's programmatic agenda—an agenda which not only involves all peoples of the earth but also encompasses all regions of the earth."[1]

The overall message of the Prophets is thus ultimately positive and reaches all the way to the New Testament. Despite opposition from all quarters and the sin of His people, God's saving purposes continue to advance in history as the anticipated Messiah and His kingdom draw nearer.

This brings us to the last characteristic of a prophetic book, the personal nature of its message. The prophets address themselves not only to their original audiences but to us, for they ultimately spoke of the gospel (1 Peter 1:10–12). For all their audiences, the prophets' message was intended to bring about profound change in the hearer as God accomplished His saving work through His word. The prophets promote change in countless ways, but the essence of the change is easy to summarize. The prophets spur their hearers and readers to follow the Lord fully here and now considering the future fulfillment of His twin works of salvation and judgment.

This response begins as we take God's word with utmost seriousness, submitting ourselves to Him and to it. Repentance is at the heart of this response and is a constant turning from sin

---

1. Paul R. Williamson, "Promise and Fulfillment: The Territorial Inheritance," in *The Land of Promise: Biblical, Theological and Contemporary Perspectives*, ed. P. Johnston and P. Walker (Downers Grove, Ill.: InterVarsity, 2000), 22.

and our old nature to God as He has revealed Himself in Jesus Christ. The prophets routinely address heart issues: How do we see ourselves? What do we love? In what or in whom do we seek satisfaction? On what is our hope based? At the same time, the prophetic books present God in all His glory as the one who loves, pardons, adopts, transforms, sanctifies, and will eventually bring His people into the full enjoyment of His completed work of salvation.

What Is an Old Testament Prophet?

This inevitably soaring description of the content of the prophetic books contrasts sharply with the experience of the prophets themselves. Called by God to be the primary means through which He communicated His will to His people, Moses and many prophets accepted this call to speak on behalf of God to the Israelites, to Israel's leaders, and occasionally to non-Israelites, as Jonah reminds us. The prophets' audiences were typically not very open to their message of judgment and calls to repentance. Content with their lives as they were, living on their own terms, both commoners and rulers were apt to reject and even threaten or persecute true prophets (Jer. 26; 37:11–15; 38:1–6; Amos 7:10–17; Mic. 2:6). False prophets, on the other hand, could make a nice living by telling people what they wanted to hear and claiming to speak for God as they did so (Mic. 3:5–7).

The role of covenant prosecutor, and the related role of herald of future judgment and salvation, made the prophetic task both challenging and profoundly important. The prophets clearly viewed their office this way and used their God-given gifts and skills to formulate their messages as powerfully as possible. Amos recounts Israel's repeated nonresponse to God's discipline as a preface to the bracing call to prepare to meet God (Amos 4:12); Nahum mocks and taunts an empire whose pride was boundless (Nahum 3); Habakkuk includes his own dialogue with God as the substance of his book; and Zephaniah describes in graphic terms the violent nature of God's wrath against sin. These and many other ways of surprising, confronting, challenging, imploring, threatening, encouraging, and promising are part of the prophetic repertoire of provoking the response of repentance. As the ultimate intended audience of the prophets (1 Peter 1:12), we must listen to them with humility and with the prayer that God's grace would enable us to respond as we ought to this Spirit-conveyed word that is spirit and life (John 6:63).

The Seventh-Century BC Prophets

The placement of the books of Nahum, Habakkuk, and Zephaniah toward the end of the Minor Prophets reflects their connection to the seventh-century BC context during which these three prophets were active in Judah. Micah's and Isaiah's ministries ended near the end of the eighth century (Mic. 1:1), and only the beginning of Jeremiah's ministry overlapped with the ministries of Habakkuk and Zephaniah. The other three minor prophets—Haggai, Zechariah, and Malachi—were active some seventy-five years or more later, after Judah had been conquered by Babylon and once the return from exile had begun.

The seventh-century ministries of Nahum, Habakkuk, and Zephaniah were both difficult and significant. The Northern Kingdom of Israel had fallen to Assyria in 722 after two centuries of worsening unfaithfulness to the covenant. This proof of God's justice and the seriousness of sin should have prompted reform and renewal in the Southern Kingdom but almost never did so. At the same time, however, the evident power and prestige of Assyria led some Judeans to either trust in Assyria for security or to conclude that God was not involved in the affairs of His people, who were threatened by that polytheistic empire. When Babylon's rise began near the end of the seventh century, that empire too provoked questions about God's wisdom and justice in using them to administer covenant discipline and eventually destroy Judah.

Confronted with these problems, the seventh-century prophets regularly spoke against trust in other nations and pressed God's people to repent of their sin and turn back to God, trusting that He would deal with Judah's enemies in due time. Each of these emphases is present as a theme in the books of Nahum, Habakkuk, and Zephaniah. Their critiques of Assyria and Babylon reveal that these empires were much more than military states. They were above all expressions of a sinful will to dominate God's world and to usurp His roles of universal King and Judge. Even though God had used Assyria to punish Israel, its pride and excesses in doing so made it ripe for judgment (see Zeph. 2:13–15), and the same would be true of Babylon (see Hab. 2:6–20). These prophets' oracles against the nations are thus assertions of God's absolute supremacy and a caution against trusting in earthly power for deliverance or security.

Despite such warnings, the foreign policy of the Judean king Manasseh was marked by trust in Assyria and the rejection of Yahweh in favor of other (false) gods. This infidelity seems to have become widespread in Judah, and Habakkuk and Zephaniah speak vehemently against those who act contrary to God's law. At the same time, the prophets' distinction between the faithful and the unfaithful in Judah brings increasing clarity to the concept of the remnant within Judah, which is characterized by humility, obedience, and trust in God.

The message of Nahum, Habakkuk, and Zephaniah announces to God's people that they are responsible to Him in the bonds of the covenant and calls them to repentance. Although God uses nations like Assyria to punish His people, this must not be understood as proof of these nations' unparalleled power or ability to provide absolute security. The seventh-century prophets portray the full salvation that God will bring in such a way that all these issues are addressed. His judgment of Judah at the hands of the nations will purify His people, and He will eventually repay the nations for their pride, idolatry, and violence. This judgment-deliverance goes far beyond the fall of Assyria and Babylon and the return of the exiles, and the remnant can look forward to the day when God will eliminate all evil and consummate His rule and His relationship with His people.

> The LORD your God in your midst,
> The Mighty One, will save;
> He will rejoice over you with gladness,
> He will quiet you with His love,
> He will rejoice over you with singing. (Zeph. 3:17)

Resources

Gentry, Peter. *How to Read and Understand the Biblical Proph-
       ets*. Wheaton, Ill.: Crossway, 2017. 144 pp. A short but
       insightful overview of the theology and particularities of
       prophetic books.

Goldsworthy, Graeme. *According to Plan: The Unfolding Revelation
       of God in the Bible*. Downers Grove, Ill.: InterVarsity, 1991.
       251 pp. A very clear overview of redemptive history—the
       tracing of God's plan, promises, and covenants from cre-
       ation to new creation.

Hughes, Philip E. *Interpreting Prophecy: An Essay in Biblical Perspec-
       tives*. Grand Rapids: Eerdmans, 1976. 135 pp. A concise,
       clear discussion of how the Bible's pieces fit together
       (e.g., Old Testament in the New Testament, typology,
       fulfillment).

Robertson, O. Palmer. *The Christ of the Prophets*. Phillipsburg,
       N.J.: P&R, 2004. 417 pp. A thorough introduction to the
       historical backgrounds, content, and theology of the pro-
       phetic books.

CHAPTER 1

Judgment and Salvation

Nahum 1:2–8

At first glance the book of Nahum would seem to have little to do with the overall message of the Bible and particularly with the message of the coming of God's kingdom and redemption from sin in Jesus Christ. After all, what importance can the fall of an ancient empire have beside the rather simple fact that its fall fulfills various biblical prophecies against it? Further, how does a message almost entirely focused on destruction contribute to the Bible's salvation-focused story line?

These questions and others draw attention to some of the challenges that face readers of Nahum. But these questions are not without answers, and Nahum's themes do indeed intersect and connect to major themes in the Old Testament that, when fully developed in the New Testament, are inseparable from salvation through Christ and God's triumph over evil and all His enemies. We will first study Nahum 1:2–8, which serves as the backdrop for the Assyria-focused material that follows. We will then explore Nahum's condemnation of Nineveh and Assyria, noting how it guides the reader toward a theological rather than a national or political definition of God's enemies. Along the way we will see how God's judgment of His and His people's enemies serves the ultimate goal of their deliverance.

Historical Background

One word summarizes the historical background of Nahum: *Assyria*. This empire, centered in upper Mesopotamia (northern portions of modern-day Iran and Iraq), had existed for well over one thousand years before Israel arrived on the scene in the Levant (the eastern Mediterranean region, including modern-day Israel and Palestinian territories, Jordan, Syria, and parts of Egypt, Iraq, and Turkey). After several ups and downs, Assyria became the dominant power in the ancient Near East by the end of the ninth century BC. By that time the united monarchy of Israel, ruled first by David and then Solomon, had separated into the Northern Kingdom of Israel and the much smaller Southern Kingdom of Judah. The north quickly veered into idolatrous worship under Jeroboam I (930–909; see 1 Kings 12) and into worship of other gods under Ahab in particular (873–852).[1] The south, home to the temple and the Davidic monarchy, was blessed with more faithful kings, especially Asa (911–870), Jotham (758–743), Hezekiah (727–698), and Josiah (639–609), and its descent into covenant infidelity was slower.

The occasional reports of Assyrian aggression against Judah, for example during the reign of Hezekiah (see 2 Kings 18–19; Isaiah 36–37), bear witness to Assyria's rapid expansion from its homeland, first westward and then southward toward Judah. Although Assyrian imperial ideology held that the expansion of the empire was necessary and even inevitable because of the support that the Assyrian gods gave to the king, more practical reasons were also at work. These included the need for

---

1. All dates are from Iain Provan, V. Philips Long, and Tremper Longman III, *A Biblical History of Israel*, 2nd ed. (Louisville, Ky.: Westminster/John Knox, 2015), 328.

natural resources such as lumber and metals, which were in short supply in upper Mesopotamia, as well as manpower and precious metals.[2]

To facilitate its growth, Assyria developed an unusually violent approach to warfare to intimidate its intended targets into submission and so avoid lengthy and costly wars. As an example, Ashurnasirpal II (883–859) summarizes one of his campaigns in these grisly terms: "While I was in the city of Aribua, I conquered the cities of the land of Laḫutu. I killed many of them (i.e., the inhabitants). I demolished, I destroyed; I burnt with fire. I captured soldiers alive by hand. I impaled (them) on stakes in front of their cities."[3]

This brutal and relentless expansion that continued almost uninterrupted from the late tenth century until the middle of the seventh century was driven by two interrelated ideas. First, the gods of Assyria, and especially the national god Assur, laid claim to the entire world. Second, the king, chosen and empowered by these gods, was responsible for bringing this plan to reality by expanding Assyria's control as far as possible. These beliefs made Assyrian foreign policy a thoroughly theological affair. Note how Ashurnasirpal, adopting a style that continued almost unchanged for centuries, describes himself and the imperial mission:

---

2. A. Kirk Grayson, "Assyrian Civilization," in *Cambridge Ancient History*, vol. 3, part 2, *The Assyrian and Babylonian Empires and Other States of the Near East, from the Eighth to the Sixth Centuries B.C.*, ed. J. Boardman et al. (Cambridge: Cambridge University Press, 1991), 214.

3. Brent Strawn, "Ashurnasirpal II," in *The Ancient Near East: Historical Sources in Translation*, ed. Mark W. Chavalas (Oxford: Blackwell, 2006), 288.

(I am) Ashurnasirpal (II), strong king, king of the world,
king without rival, king of all the four quarters (of the world),
divine sun of all the people,... divine weapon of the great
gods,... who is fearless (in) combat, high flood-wave that has
no opponent,... the one who walks upon the necks of his
foes, who tramples all enemies, who scatters the band of the
arrogant, who moves about with the help of the great gods,
his lords, and whose hand has conquered all lands.[4]

Assyria was thus a massively powerful, terribly violent,
economically and religiously motivated empire focused on sub-
jugating the known world for the glory of its gods and the good
of the empire itself. As the quotations above suggest, it was a law
unto itself, with might making right. By Nahum's day, Judah had
already suffered from significant Assyrian aggression, like when
Sennacherib destroyed dozens of fortified towns in his unsuccessful bid to conquer Judah in 701 BC or when Judah became
Assyria's vassal during the reign of Manasseh. This vassal relationship required Judah to pay taxes to Assyria, contribute
Judean soldiers to Assyria's wars, and swear fidelity to Assyria.

From the biblical point of view, this was not entirely unexpected since Judah's fidelity to God often wavered, especially
under the leadership of unbelieving kings like Ahaz (743–714)
and Manasseh (698–642). Nonetheless, the way Assyria dealt
with Judah and especially the pride that flowered as it exercised
its violence and supremacy were extreme expressions of sin and
disdain for God (Isaiah 10). This pattern of behavior, some two
hundred years old by the time Nahum prophesied, made Assyria
ripe for judgment, even more so because Jonah's exceptional mission to Nineveh had produced no lasting results. This brings us

---

4. Strawn, "Ashurnasirpal II," 287.

to the first verse of the book, which introduces Nahum's message as having to do with Nineveh and by extension with Assyria.

Judgment and Salvation as the Big Picture
Although the first verse of Nahum identifies its subject as Nineveh, the capital city of the Assyrian Empire from 705 BC until the fall of the empire a century later, the first section (1:2–8) says nothing at all about Nineveh or Assyria. In fact, no nation or people group is mentioned. Instead of such particulars, this poem takes the widest possible perspective on the issue addressed by Nahum's prophecy of Assyria's fall later in the book: God will act decisively in the future, putting an end to evil and those who practice it while delivering those who seek refuge in Him. It is thus a powerful and concise summary of the entire biblical story line, but it also brings these central truths to bear on the reader. All humanity stands guilty before God, yet He graciously holds out the possibility of salvation in Him alone. A response of repentance and trust in Yahweh's gracious offer of salvation is thus the only sensible response in the face of His future judgment.

God's Vengeance in the Foreground, Grace Visible in the Background
The first verse of Nahum's first section, an acrostic poem that uses exactly one-half of the twenty-two letters of the Hebrew alphabet, is one of the more repetitive theological statements in the Bible. Not only does it assert three times that God takes vengeance, but it adds that in His vengeance He is "jealous" and "furious" (v. 2). Nothing else is mentioned in this verse other than that God's "adversaries" and "enemies" are those against whom He will take vengeance. This provides a very strong, highly focused

introduction to what the book of Nahum is about. It also does all but state outright that divine vengeance is the primary theme of the book. But this compact theological statement is not blunt or without finesse, for it limits the exercise of divine vengeance to God's enemies and adversaries.

This hint at the possibility of mercy for others is confirmed by the contrasting affirmation in verse 3 that God is "slow to anger." This short phrase is potent, and even more so when the reader recognizes it as an echo of God's self-revelation to Moses in Exodus 34:6. This verse comes near the end of a section that interrupts the instructions for the building and operation of the tabernacle. Israel, recently liberated from slavery in Egypt and delivered from its clutches in the most spectacular manner, now finds itself at Mount Sinai. Reminded of this stunning deliverance, the nation has committed to a relationship of obedience to God its Savior (Ex. 19:4–8). God's full revelation of the covenant's content in the following chapters has met with Israel's formal acceptance of the covenant in Exodus 24:3–8, after which Moses ascended Mount Sinai with Joshua to receive the tablets on which God would write the law and the commandments for them (34:28).

The Relevance of God's Character and Past Actions for the Present and Future

This sequence of events, in which God fulfilled His promise to Abraham to bring his descendants out of slavery (Gen. 15:13–14) and Israel was visited by God Himself and entered a covenant with Him, was violently interrupted by Israel's decision to abandon God and Moses in favor of gods whom Aaron, their new leader, would make for them (Ex. 32:1). Astonishingly, Aaron complies with their demand, although he tries to connect their worship of false gods with Yahweh (v. 5). It is at this point that God tells Moses that "your people…have corrupted themselves" and "turned aside" (vv. 7–8) from following Him, in direct violation of the solemn oath they had so recently taken when they entered the covenant. This infidelity is so serious that God's wrath threatens to destroy the entire nation, Moses excepted (vv. 9–14). Only when Moses intercedes does God relent and limit His most severe punishment to a small part of the nation (vv. 25–29) while sending a plague among the people (v. 35).

Despite these measures, the larger issue of God's presence among His people, which was to have been by means of the tabernacle introduced in Exodus 25, has not yet been resolved. Only after further intercession by Moses for this rebellious people does God agree to continue with His people on the way to Canaan. It is this chain of profoundly gracious and clement divine responses to Israel's apostasy that lies behind the statement that Nahum 1:3 quotes from Exodus 34, where God reveals His sovereignly gracious character to Moses: "And the LORD passed before him and proclaimed, 'The LORD, the LORD God, merciful and gracious, longsuffering [literally, "slow to anger"], and abounding in goodness and truth, keeping mercy for thousands, forgiving iniquity and transgression and sin, by no means clearing the guilty'" (vv. 6–7).

Nahum's "slow to anger" (1:3) thus draws on the preeminent example of divine patience in a section that has depicted with equal power God's commitment to punish His enemies. This note of possible deliverance is reinforced by the phrase "great [or mighty] in power," which consistently refers to God's intervention on behalf of His people (see Ex. 32:11; Deut. 4:37; 9:29;

2 Kings 17:36).[5] This helps us see that the first few verses of this poem present the two main themes that run through the book. Although judgment predominates, it contributes to and is inseparable from the theme of deliverance that reaches beyond Judah (Nah. 1:12) to other nations (3:19).

A Message of Judgment with Two Possible Outcomes
With this theological foundation in place, the rest of the passage reveals that God is coming to judge the earth—that is, every human being (Nah. 1:5). His overwhelming glory will destabilize the earth itself, and His justice threatens to annihilate all without exception:

> The LORD has His way
> In the whirlwind and in the storm,
> And the clouds are the dust of His feet....
> The mountains quake before Him,
> The hills melt,
> And the earth heaves at His presence. (vv. 3, 5)

But here the earlier possibility of deliverance, hinted at by "slow to anger and great in power," comes fully into view—to the great relief of the reader! As was the case at Mount Sinai, the possibility of deliverance exists only because God delights to show grace. Here, the text attributes this possibility simply to God being "good" (v. 7), a term that Exodus 33:19 ties directly to the attributes that God uses to describe Himself in Exodus 34:6–7. God's very character makes possible the deliverance of those who trust in Him.

---

5. Daniel C. Timmer, *Nahum: A Discourse Analysis of the Hebrew Bible*, Zondervan Exegetical Commentary on the Old Testament 30 (Grand Rapids: Zondervan Academic, 2020), 79–80.

The point of Nahum's message is clear and confronts the reader with an all-important question: "Who can stand" (v. 6) before this God when He comes in vengeance against His enemies? Nahum also guides the reader toward one of two mutually exclusive answers to that question: only those who "trust in" (v. 7) God ("take refuge in," ESV) will survive this judgment. They will not survive because they are innocent, for then no trust in God's mercy would be necessary. Rather, as every Israelite should have known, deliverance from sin's consequences was freely available through the sacrificial system, in which the life of an animal was accepted in place of the life of the sinner. Reconciliation with God, then as now, requires that sinners recognize their sin and the divine condemnation under which they find themselves and turn from that sin to the God who offers forgiveness and life in all its fullness to those who trust in His promise of salvation. Only one other response and one other outcome are possible. Those who will not recognize their guilt before God or who would reject His absolute authority over them remain His enemies. They will, when their enmity exhausts God's patience (Rom. 9:22), be overcome by His just judgment and unable to save themselves.

The first section of the book of Nahum, focusing on God's vengeance but gradually revealing the only possible way of escape from the terrifying judgment that threatens the unrepentant, is a rich and powerful meditation on God's attributes and character. Its strong emphasis on God's vengeance sets in bold relief the undeserved and unexpected mercy and goodness of God to sinners. Indeed, we see God's goodness only as we see our need for that goodness—as we see our sin. Despite its emphasis on divine wrath, Nahum's theology is far from negative or discouraging in its intent. As we see how radically (i.e., to the root) sin affects and corrupts us, we will see the glory and incomprehensibility of God's goodness as He offers salvation through Jesus Christ. This salvation is glorious because it is precisely what we need, and it is the only solution to the grave dilemma in which we sinners find ourselves. God's mercy in Christ is incomprehensible for many reasons, not least of which is that God Himself makes salvation possible and invites sinners to come to Him for it— even though it is against Him that we have sinned.

The Bible is full of responses to this glorious salvation, and even in the Old Testament, believers were overwhelmed by its glory and confident in its reality in the present and in the future. The effects of this salvation can hardly be summarized: believers are "glad" (Ps. 16:9), trust that God will see them through every trial and provide all that they need (Psalm 23), learn from Him (25:8), fear nothing (27:1), call to Him for help (28:1), take refuge in Him (31:1 ESV, the same term as Nah. 1:7 ESV), and are ready to praise Him at all times (Ps. 34:1). This chorus of praise will continue eternally when God's people have entered His heavenly courts (Rev. 15:3–4).

Questions for Reflection

1. How does the global perspective on God's justice and mercy in Nahum 1:2–8 set the stage for what follows in the rest of the book?

2. How do God's vengeance and mercy fit together in Nahum's exhortation to the reader to seek refuge in God?

3. How can you respond more often and more profoundly to the goodness of God in salvation, both what you have experienced so far and what God promises He will one day give you in its fullness?

Resources

Packer, J. I. *Knowing God*. Downers Grove, Ill.: InterVarsity, 1973. 287 pp. A stellar and practical treatment of God's attributes and more. See especially chapter 16, "Goodness and Severity" (158–66).

Piper, John. *Providence*. Wheaton, Ill.: Crossway, 2020. 751 pp. Note especially "Seeing and Savoring the Providence of God" (pp. 691–711).

CHAPTER 2

God's Enemy Is Not Assyria
Nahum 1:9–15

It may seem strange to say that God's enemy in most of the book of Nahum (from 1:9 onward) is not Assyria. After all, the first verse says that Nahum's message concerns Nineveh, and much of the book focuses on this city, its defenders, and on Assyria's king and the elites who serve in his administration. As we will see, however, God's critique of Assyria is very carefully focused, and although the judgment announced against Assyria does involve its conquest by a foreign power (Babylon), these events were of significance mainly for those who were at the head of the empire and the armed forces who were to defend them. This means that the general population did not suffer the same punishments as those who promoted the empire's ideology and usurped divine glory and prerogative in doing so.

It also shows that God's enemies are not identified by race or nationality but by what they think of themselves and of God. Pride, using resources and even other people in ways that advance personal interests, and ignoring God's glory and authority meet with severe consequences in Nahum, but these evils are not found only in empires. God's condemnation of Assyria's leaders is applicable to individuals, political parties, and any group who acts in these ways, seeking to define and realize its own destiny by whatever means and power it has. In short, God judges those who refuse to live under His beneficent rule and pursue autonomy apart from Him, whether individuals or groups. In this section we will trace the radically different ways that God commits to acting toward proud, rebellious Assyria (with a focus on its ideology and leaders) and toward Judah, which is defined not as the Southern Kingdom without any nuance but as those who trust in God's deliverance and will praise Him for it.

Against Assyria

The first words addressed to Assyria (Nah. 1:9–11) assert that this empire plotted not only against Judah but against God Himself in its attempts to control the eastern Mediterranean. As we saw earlier, Assyria's imperial ideology held that the empire's gods were on their side because the Assyrians were fulfilling the divine mandate to subjugate the world to their god Assur in particular. As a result, their foreign policy was thoroughly religious and theological. The conversation between the Assyrian Rabshakeh and Hezekiah's men in 2 Kings 18 makes this very clear and is probably referred to in verse 11: "one who plots evil against the LORD, a wicked counselor."

Dismissing Judah's trust in Egypt and even in God as useless, the Assyrian cohort announces that just as no other nation's gods have been able to deliver them from Assyria's power, so Judah and its God will be conquered by the Assyrians (2 Kings 18). The Lord's response in 2 Kings 19 rebuts these Assyrian claims on the same level. Condemning the Assyrian king's pride, God asserts that what He has done has been possible only because He ordained it long ago. More pointedly, the Lord will nullify the king's boasts against Him and His people by sending the ruler back to Assyria, where he eventually will be killed by his sons in a failed coup attempt (2 Kings 19:28, 36–37). This history is well known to Nahum and his audience, and here God asserts some fifty years later that He will once and for all end the line of Assyrian kings and show that their pride was groundless.

God's second speech to Assyria in verse 14 is addressed directly to the king as the one who exemplifies and enacts Assyria's godless, violent, and proud project of world domination. This verse draws a radical contrast between two kings. The Lord as King of creation utters a decree that negates and condemns the claims and plans of the Assyrian king, showing by that simple act that there is only one King who can speak with authority and who can raise up and bring down kings and kingdoms (Dan. 2:21). God first announces the end of the Assyrian monarch's name, meaning his reputation in the present and his legacy after his death: "Your name shall be perpetuated no longer" (Nah. 1:14). God promises to destroy the cult statues, those which the king worships and which were thought to channel the gods to whom they belong: "Out of the house of your gods I will cut off the carved image and the molded image" (v. 14). In the ancient Near East, this action would normally be taboo because a conquering army did not want to incur the wrath of the gods of the people it conquered. But it carries no taboo for the Lord, who knows and who will demonstrate that these so-called gods are really nothing. Finally, the Assyrian king will die and be buried, putting an absolute end to his claims and designs and proving that he is in the end "vile" (or insignificant).[1]

---

1. Daniel C. Timmer, "Nahum," in *Daniel–Malachi*, vol. 7 of ESV Expository Commentary, ed. Jay Sklar, Iain M. Duguid, and James M. Hamilton Jr. (Wheaton, Ill.: Crossway, 2018), 517.

For Judah

Judah in Assyria is not assumed to be perfect—it has, until now, been under divine discipline (Nah. 1:12). Nonetheless, God's covenant commitments to His people are such that He will not leave them indefinitely in distress. As was the case with Assyria, God speaks directly to His people twice, beginning in verses 12–13. The first message is simple but very welcome news. Despite Assyria's obviously superior strength, Judah will be liberated when Assyria is "cut down" (v. 12). Considering this coming deliverance, God commands Judah to prepare to celebrate its festivals, whether Passover, Weeks, or Booths, and to pay the vows that had been made together with prayers for deliverance. Like the Judeans' vows, their feasts celebrated God's past deliverance and provision. Following the fall of Assyria, Judeans could celebrate them with new zeal, having seen with their own eyes new proofs of God's saving purposes for His people.

We have already seen the connection between Nahum's message against Assyria and the gospel by noting that God's enemies then and now, whether individuals or groups of one sort or another, have in common spite for God and His authority, an inflated sense of self-importance, and the firm intention to live by their own rules for their own purposes. The echo of Isaiah 52:1, 7 in Nahum 1:15 adds a complementary perspective that highlights deliverance rather than judgment. In the book of Isaiah, chapter 52 follows God's earlier assertion to the exiles that His wrath against them has come to an end and introduces a powerful and far-reaching description of all that God will do for His people as He restores them from exile and ultimately purifies them from sin through the work of the Suffering Servant (Isaiah 53). This section of Isaiah closes with a call to jubilant praise of God as the husband and Holy One of His people who will fully deliver them from sin and danger and bring them into a perfected paradise (Isaiah 54–55).

Why does Nahum draw on this text if Judah's deliverance is merely political? Because even though the fall of Assyria is not the end of exile (which would occur later) nor, far less, was it the full realization of God's saving purposes for His people, it was a demonstration of His faithfulness to those covenantal purposes and a partial realization of them. What is more, this partial fulfillment directs the faith of Nahum's readers beyond the fall of Assyria to the full salvation that Isaiah foresees and describes.[2]

Nahum's Message and the Rest of the Bible

These two perspectives should guide believers' responses to the message of Nahum, their interpretation of current events, and their hopes for the future. With respect to the world around us, Nahum shows that the church's enemies cannot be equated woodenly with particular nations or political parties, even though such agglomerations of power may promote ideals or act in ways that militate against God, His will, and His people. The temptation to identify God's enemies directly with particular groups was not even possible in Nahum, since the divine critique focused on a small group of Assyrians who were fully committed to promoting a worldview directed against God Himself. And even then, God's judgment included the so-called gods that these people used to advance their agendas. Ultimately, God opposes not only sinners but especially demonic forces that animate such opposition.

---

2. Daniel C. Timmer, "Nahum, Book of," in *Dictionary of the New Testament Use of the Old Testament*, ed. G. K. Beale et al. (Grand Rapids: Baker Academic, forthcoming 2023).

It is understandable that the church looks outside itself for such enemies, and indeed they are often outside its ranks. Yet the letters to the churches in Revelation remind us that the church is not beyond the influence of such powers. This influence may produce moral laxity (Rev. 2:14, 20), sloth (3:1–2), lukewarmness (3:15–17), or other vices. Even sins as mundane as anger (Eph. 4:26) and pride (1 Tim. 3:6) can weaken and sicken the body of Christ. As Paul teaches in Ephesians 6, the Christian is required to wage spiritual warfare with diligence, constant prayer, and the proper means: truth, righteousness, gospel peace, faith, confidence in God's sure salvation, and the sword of His word.

Amid this struggle, God's promises of our final victory in and through the victory of Jesus Christ on our behalf sustain our faith. It is for good reason that immediately following the letters to the churches in Revelation, John is allowed to glance into heaven itself, where he sees God Almighty seated on His throne (Rev. 4:2–3), surrounded by heavenly hosts and worshiped without ceasing as the one who has created and rules all things (vv. 8, 11). The same vision then focuses on the Lion of the tribe of Judah, who has "prevailed" and will fully apply His saving work (5:5–10). Whatever enemies array themselves against God, be they as powerful as Assyria in Nahum's day or as crafty and massive as Babylon and other powers in Revelation, they will never impede God or His purposes. Much like Assyria's fall brings relief and liberty to Judah in the book of Nahum, the final destruction of God's enemies in the marriage supper of the Lamb (Revelation 19) leads to the full salvation of God's people in the new heaven and the new earth (Revelation 21–22). Nahum calls us to look forward to this glorious day in sober trust and with great anticipation.

Questions for Reflection

1. What elements or people in Assyria does Nahum critique? How does this make Assyria a "theological" entity, and how does that affect the interpretation of the book?

2. What similarities do you see between Assyria's ideology and imperialism and individual sins and attitudes in your life (such as pride, the ends justifying the means, lack of dependence on God)?

3. Read the description of Babylon and its fall in Revelation 17:1–19:10, then think of ways that the same priorities, beliefs, and practices might be present in cultural, religious, or other nonpolitical spheres.

Resources

Bauckham, Richard. *The Theology of the Book of Revelation.* Cambridge: Cambridge University Press, 1993. 184 pp. A brief and very helpful exposition of the theology of Revelation.

Bridges, Jerry. *Respectable Sins.* Colorado Springs, Colo.: NavPress, 2007. 288 pp. A pastoral exploration of sins we commonly live comfortably with, such as anxiety, discontentment, and anger, among others.

Gladd, Benjamin L., and Matthew S. Harmon. *Making All Things New: Inaugurated Eschatology for the Life of the Church.* Grand Rapids: Baker Academic, 2016. 224 pp. A wide-ranging reflection on how believers should live and serve in the already–not yet tension of the time between Christ's first and second comings.

Hendrickson, William. *More Than Conquerors: An Interpretation of the Book of Revelation.* Grand Rapids: Baker, 1988. 240 pp. A clear, practical explanation of Revelation.

Hoekema, Anthony A. *The Bible and the Future.* Grand Rapids: Eerdmans, 1979. 354 pp. A thorough study of biblical prophecy and eschatology.

CHAPTER 3

The Judgment of Nineveh
Nahum 2

Nahum 2 includes a detailed vision of Nineveh's fall in verses 1–10 and a short speech by God that interprets that event in the last three verses. The mocking tone exhibited occasionally in chapter 1 (see vv. 10–11, 14) is also present in this chapter, reinforced by several images that show the undoing or failure of the very things that Assyria and Nineveh thought were guarantees of their permanence and inviolability. This debunking of the empire's claims reaches its peak in the divine speech of verses 11–13, where God affirms that He will destroy Assyria in terms that Assyria itself used to describe its dominance and violence against the nations it conquered.

The Fall of Nineveh Foreseen
Chapter 2 begins with the prophet seemingly warning Nineveh to prepare for an attack. But the vision reveals that all preparations will be unsuccessful in preserving Nineveh from destruction. Verse 2 reminds the reader that Nineveh's fall is essential to Judah's restoration since God's purposes of judgment and salvation cannot be separated. If there is an echo of Genesis 32 here, this reminder presumes that the "Jacob" who will benefit from the fall of Assyria has learned to trust in God and depend

on His gracious blessing rather than on its own strength, as Jacob himself learned when he wrestled with God (Gen. 32:26).

This emphasis on the necessity of faith aligns nicely with what the entire chapter presupposes: that Assyria trusts in its own strategies, gods, alliances, plans validated by divination, and brute strength to protect itself against all attacks. Assyria's misplaced faith is slowly but surely undone in this section as the reader follows the attacker from outside the city toward its center, and finally to its humiliated and conquered inhabitants. Along the way, almost every element of Nineveh's defensive forces and infrastructure is mentioned, with the crucially important fact that none of them can stop the steady progress of the enemy. The fall of Nineveh shows, one step at a time, that Assyria's faith in its gods and itself was utterly unwarranted.

After the initial call for Nineveh to prepare for battle, the scene shifts to the attacking army, which arrives in impressive colors and with evident preparation (Nah. 2:3). In contrast to the Medo-Babylonian army's chariots, which rush around the city without impediment, the Assyrian officers stumble in their vain attempt to defend the city's massive walls:

> He remembers his nobles;
> They stumble in their walk;
> They make haste to her walls,
> And the defense is prepared. (v. 5)

The elaborate waterworks meant to embellish and irrigate the gardens at the heart of the city now symbolize the flood of destruction that overruns even the citadel at the city's center and the palaces and temples that stood there. The cult statue, the "she" of verse 7, was probably of Ishtar, a female deity associated especially with war. Ironically, this bellicose deity is defeated and stripped of her cult ornaments, effectively announcing that she is defunct and unable to save Nineveh despite being particularly important to it (some seventh-century BC Assyrian texts refer to Ishtar as the "Lady of Nineveh").[1]

At this point it is already evident that Nineveh will never rise again, and it is compared to a pool or basin of water that has cracked and will soon contain no water at all. The motif of emptying also appears in the description of the sacking of the city, which had amassed an enormous quantity of material wealth over several centuries, especially in the form of spoils of war. The irony is again rich: the city that had profited by taking by force what belonged to others is now despoiled and left empty. Indeed, all that remains of Nineveh will be a huddled mass of defeated Assyrians, whose posture and faces reveal their utter desolation and shattered confidence in their invincibility.

Seeing Assyria, Seeing Ourselves

The point of this detailed and interpretative vision of Nineveh's fall is quite simple: Nineveh was not what it thought it was! Even more important is the why: believing themselves to be masters of their own destiny, those who held to the empire's ideology and placed their trust in the monarch and the gods they served were shown to be completely mistaken. In the theology of Nahum and the Bible in general, how could it be otherwise? Beginning with Adam and Eve's first attempt at human autonomy and self-determination (Gen. 3:6), attempts to relegate God to second place, or no place at all, inevitably fail. Furthermore, such

---

1. Barbara N. Porter, "Ishtar of Nineveh and Her Collaborator, Ishtar of Arbela, in the Reign of Assurbanipal," *Iraq* 66 (2004): 41.

grasping after divine prerogatives and authority has the terribly ironic result of bringing death to those who are pursuing life on their own terms.

It is all too easy for us to recognize these grave sins in empires like Assyria or in paradigmatic cases of sin like Adam's in Genesis 3 or David's in 2 Samuel 11. But every time people sin, whether they are believers or not, they are effectively saying to God, "I know what is best in this case." It is hard for us who do such things to properly gauge the arrogance and inanity of these attitudes, so self-examination and dependence on God's grace is an essential part of life with God. We must pray with David:

> Search me, O God, and know my heart;
> Try me, and know my anxieties;
> And see if there is any wicked way in me,
> And lead me in the way everlasting. (Ps. 139:23–24)

An essential part of a proper response to such pride is a renewed awareness of God's majesty and wisdom on the one hand, and an honest, frank confession of our own self-focused, self-measured, self-determined moral reckoning on the other hand. The apostle Paul calls us to just this sort of holistic, radical reformation of our entire person in Romans 12:1–2: "I beseech you therefore, brethren, by the mercies of God, that you present your bodies a living sacrifice, holy, acceptable to God, which is your reasonable service. And do not be conformed to this world, but be transformed by the renewing of your mind, that you may prove what is that good and acceptable and perfect will of God." Our whole self is to be continuously presented as a sacrifice in an act of worship that submits our mind, will, heart, strength, and abilities to God out of gratitude for the immeasurable gift of salvation in Jesus Christ. This involves the renewing of our minds by the power of the Holy Spirit so that we might increasingly know and do the will of God in every area of our lives. A sober, humble evaluation of ourselves will also prepare us for effective service in the body of Christ, using the gifts He has given us for the good of others (Rom. 12:3–8).

The Hunter Becomes the Hunted

Although it might not appear at first glance, Nahum 2:12–14 is a highly ironic, even sarcastic, slap in the face of Assyria's king. The lion at the center of this passage is none other than the Assyrian monarch. From the twelfth century BC onward, Assyrian rulers had referred to themselves as lions or as lion hunters in their royal annals, self-glorifying historical records focused on the king as warrior and divinely supported ruler.[2] These comparisons of themselves to lions were potent assertions of their courage and power in battle, where (according to the king's account) he fearlessly and irresistibly defeated his and Assyria's enemies with his army in tow.

A contrasting use of the lion theme, in which Assyria's enemies were depicted as dangerous lions that threatened the king's flock of citizens, was also common in Assyria. In this imagery, the king took on the role of the shepherd as lion hunter, wiser and more powerful than any lion and thus able to eliminate threats against his people and establishing the order that Assyria sought to impose on the world. This image was made very real by means of ritual lion hunts held in an arena in Nineveh in the last few centuries of Assyria's existence. Caged lions would be

---

2. Elena Cassin, "Le roi et le lion," *Revue de l'histoire des religions* 198 (1981): 355–401.

released, and the king, mounted in a chariot and accompanied by warriors, would kill the lions and so demonstrate his superiority over them for all to see. The hunt ended with the king pouring a drink offering over the bodies of the dead lions in worship of the gods who enabled him to dominate them and his enemies alike.[3]

Nahum was familiar with these elements of Assyrian royal ideology and used them with great irony. God declares that He will do away with the king as lion, his lionesses and cubs, and even his prey, destroying him and his military infrastructure together. God is also against the king in his role as lion hunter or shepherd, for God will use the nations that Assyria intends to keep at bay to bring it down. The lion becomes the prey, and the hunter becomes the hunted.

Pride and Humility

The directness with which Yahweh confronts the Assyrian monarch, using his cherished self-image to depict his destruction, shows how firmly God sets Himself against the proud (Ps. 138:6; James 4:6). It goes without saying that the proud think they have no need of God. That tragically wrong belief is founded on another that, unless corrected, must prove fatal: the belief that God is unable to bring them down. In other words, the assertion of one's autonomy ("I can do what I want") is inseparable from the belief that no one, not even God Himself, can impose any meaningful consequences on the person ("I am beyond the reach of any authority"). In the universe that God

---

3. Michael B. Dick, "The Neo-Assyrian Lion Hunt and Yahweh's Answer to Job," *Journal of Biblical Literature* 125 (2006): 251–52.

has created, this foolish and rebellious attitude spells the doom of all who cling to it.

At the same time, as we saw in Nahum 1, God delights to be gracious to the humble (Ps. 138:6; James 4:6). Humility is rooted in honesty about ourselves before God. Our sinfulness, mortality, limited abilities, and shortsighted strategies should be more than sufficient to convince us that we are thoroughly incapable of bringing about anything that is good and of true significance apart from God's grace and blessing. If this is true regarding our everyday business (James 4:13), how much more is it true of parenting, sharing or preaching the gospel, pursuing sanctification, and knowing God? We are responsible for wise decisions and proper behavior in these and other areas, but God's action is absolutely and exclusively determinative in any situation that involves the human soul. Paul planted, others watered, but only God can bring the fruit of faith and repentance (1 Cor. 3:5–9). Even in matters of conversion and spiritual growth, humility will enable us to serve faithfully and expectantly, trusting that God will use our faithful efforts as He sees fit. This frees us from the temptation to overvalue our role and enables us to boast only in what "the exceeding grace of God" has done (2 Cor. 9:14).

Questions for Reflection

1. How does the description of Nineveh's fall target the very things in which Assyria had boasted or put its trust?

2. How would you affirm or deny the statement that pride is at the root of every sin?

3. What are some biblical ways to undermine our pride and
   foster humility? How has pride put down roots in your self-
   image, in your relationships with others, and even in your
   walk with God? What biblical truths can help you grow
   in humility?

Resources

Edwards, Jonathan. "Spiritual Pride." In vol. 1 of *The Works of Jona-
        than Edwards*, 398–404. Edinburgh: Banner of Truth,
        1974. "Spiritual Pride" is part of the larger work *Thoughts
        on the Revival of Religion in New England* (section X, part 4,
        section 1).

Lewis, C. S. *Mere Christianity*. Revised and enlarged edition. New
        York: Macmillan, 1952. 190 pp. A concise, insightful
        introduction to the Christian faith. See book 3, chapter 8,
        "The Great Sin," on pride.

Murray, Andrew. *Humility: The Beauty of Holiness*. Minneapolis:
        Bethany House, 2001. 112 pp. A classic study of humility.

Ortlund, Dane. *Gentle and Lowly: The Heart of Christ for Sinners
        and Sufferers*. Wheaton, Ill.: Crossway, 2020. 224 pp. A
        very pastoral, heart-searching meditation on Christ and
        His marvelous sufficiency for needs of all kinds.

CHAPTER 4

Misused Power, Misplaced Confidence, Triumphant Justice

Nahum 3

Nahum's final chapter deals in no uncertain terms with several of Assyria's most characteristic moral failures: its violence, its pride, and its use of others for its own ends. Speaking on behalf of God, Nahum uses three kinds of speech to condemn Assyria and dismiss the nation from the scene of world history: an announcement of woe in verses 1–7, several taunts in verses 8–17, and a final dirge that denigrates rather than lauds Assyria in verses 18–19. These different kinds of rhetoric emphatically assert God's absolute authority over Assyria, Assyria's accountability to Him, and the futility of its attempt to ensure its uninterrupted existence. The final dirge drives home the point that God's justice makes Assyria's fall inevitable while reminding the reader that this is good news for the world at large.

Sin as a "Package Deal"

God's condemnation of Assyria in Nahum 3:1–7 deals with several sins that are distinct but interrelated. The empire's violence, often lauded in the king's annals, goes together with its deceitfulness and self-importance. These three sins are features of the empire in action, meaning that its pride drives it to determine its own destiny and to realize it by any means necessary. This describes all too well the fallen human condition in general, and when political and other forms of power accompany this worldview, the results are terrible indeed. Assyria's violence was certainly effective against its enemies, whether enacted or merely threatened, but could only be exercised if Assyria thought itself to be more important than any other nation. Pride goes hand in hand with a spiteful attitude toward others, and Assyria often refers to and treats those who resist its claims on them and what belongs to them as subhuman and without significant value.

Assyria also used diplomacy, in the broad sense of the word, to compel states to submit to its oversight or to participate in its trade arrangements. The promise of the Rabshakeh to the Judeans—that if they submitted to Assyria each of them would contentedly eat from "his own vine" and "his own fig tree" (2 Kings 18:31)—is a perfect example of the rosy promises that Assyria used to draw others into the web of its empire. The actual experience of these client states was often quite different, as they were made to "pull the yoke" of taxes, forced labor, and natural resource exploitation that Assyria imposed on them. An Assyrian king from the ninth century BC records, as did many after him, that he "put all of the lands under one command and imposed upon them (a tribute of) horses, silver, gold, barley and straw, and corvée" [forced labor].[1]

As the metaphor of the prostitute in Nahum 3:4 shows, this massive intake of goods and people was for the sole purpose of satisfying and glorifying the empire, "who sells nations through her harlotries, and families through her sorceries." This is the most explicit and blatant expression of pride, in which the empire pursues its own glory. In the case of Assyria, its elevation

---

1. Mario Liverani, *Assyria: The Imperial Mission* (Winona Lake, Ind.: Eisenbrauns, 2017), 160, 162.

of itself could not take place without demeaning and almost destroying those around it, making them serve the sole purpose of glorifying it or contributing to imperial actions having this goal. It is not hard to perceive behind such actions the twisted usurpation of divine status. Assyria wanted to rule all things for its own glory and was ready to destroy all who opposed that all-important project.

Assyria's obsession with its own glory and satisfaction explains why God's response focuses on shaming the empire and uncovering the diplomatic schemes that it used to extract whatever resources it could from the nations that fell under its sway. God's justice in destroying Assyria is evident even to godless nations who had been victims of Assyria's violent empire building, for there will be no one who mourns its fall (Nah. 3:7). Those who know and trust God's justice can be sure that, even if their deliverance comes only through death (2 Tim. 4:18), God will eventually eliminate all evil and deliver His people from it.

Fitting Insults and the End of Assyria's Pride

Nahum's taunts in Nahum 3:8–17 are another means that God uses to show His people that Assyria's claims to unparalleled greatness are specious and unwarranted. These negative statements against Assyria are God's way of exposing the lies at the heart of Assyria's ideology and worldview that brought it into conflict with Him. The first taunt, in verses 8–11, begins by comparing Nineveh, with its massive walls, to No Amon (Thebes), an Egyptian city protected by the massive expanses of desert around it and whose defensive structures and mercenary defenders were as effective as a sea. Despite its very secure setting, No Amon fell quickly in 671 BC—and to Assyrian forces.

God's negative evaluation of Assyria is thus highly ironic, for Nineveh would surely have argued that it was stronger than No Amon precisely because Assyria conquered it. But that is simply irrelevant. God determines when Nineveh may thrive and when it must fall, and its time has come.

The second half of the taunt applies this truth to Assyria as a whole. God asserts that the entire land, including especially its fortified cities, is like a tree full of ripe figs that will fall into the mouth of one ready to eat them the moment that the tree is shaken. Assyria's insignificance is subtly included in the image of a human being consuming figs, which are radically less important than the one eating them and are totally unable to resist being consumed. The comparison of Assyria's armed forces with women implies that they are weaker than this attacker, who is thus unstoppable:

> Surely, your people in your midst are women!
> The gates of your land are wide open for your enemies;
> Fire shall devour the bars of your gates. (3:13)

The second taunt sarcastically calls for Assyria to prepare for a siege by drawing water and fortifying its defensive sites. Yet before it can even complete these preparations, much less engage the enemy, God tells them,

> The fire will devour you,
> The sword will cut you off;
> It will eat you up like a locust. (Nah. 3:15a)

This leads to the third taunt, which compares the empire itself to an enormous hoard of locusts that, despite its size, disappears as quickly as it arrives (vv. 15b–17). Whatever permanence Assyria had thought to have attained by military preparedness, diplomatic arrangements, and the elimination of possible threats turns out to be a mirage. In contemporary terms, whatever earthly-minded strong men, celebrities, political movements, or nations may assert of themselves and their legacies, God has promised to "shake all nations," glorifying Himself while exposing the impermanence and transience of human achievements (Hag. 2:7). A life dedicated in all its spheres to the glory of God is the only way to participate in the only "kingdom which cannot be shaken" (Heb. 12:28).

Nahum's final words are really final words, meaning that they take the form of a dirge pronounced over the deceased. Anticipating the death of the Assyrian king, this dirge repeatedly emphasizes the insignificance (recall Nah. 1:14), impotence, and imminent death of the one at the head of the Assyrian Empire's godless and reckless pursuit of power and glory. This brings the book full circle by returning to the focus on the king with which it began in 1:14 and by emphasizing the evil that summarizes the empire's beliefs and actions (recall 1:11). The positive consequences of Assyria's fall include the deliverance of the nations it had oppressed, and this reminds the reader of God's good plan for His people, as seen in 1:13, 15.

Hope through Judgment and Salvation

The last chapter of Nahum may seem far removed from Christian existence in the twenty-first century, but it surely is not. The world is full of individuals, corporations, social groups, movements, and nations that act as Assyria did. The modern condition is one that privileges the individual's feelings and desires, granting them inherent legitimacy.[2] Mixed with the "Promethean passion of modern humankind, which developed from a desire for independence to a desire for unbridled power," individuals try to "form themselves with their own hands."[3] This means that contemporary cultures habitually attempt to dethrone God and place the individual or the collective on the throne. Sadly, they all too often seem to succeed—at least in the short term.

It will not always be so. Nahum reminds us, first, that God will deal decisively with those who oppose Him once His patience is exhausted. Second, God will not abandon His church in this world nor let it be overrun. God's work of salvation and the coming of His kingdom cannot be stopped or even resisted (Matt. 16:18). These twin truths are a source of immense comfort and encouragement to Christians. However the church may appear to be doing in a particular context, it remains Christ's church, and He will rule until all His enemies have been put under His feet (1 Cor. 15:25).

No less importantly, the time between Christ's first and second comings is when the church is to take the gospel to the nations, meaning to those currently in rebellion against God, as the book of Acts repeatedly shows. Humility (we, too, were once "slaves of sin," Rom. 6:20) and love for the lost, modeled above all by God Himself, are essential if we are to fulfill this charge. With a desire to see God glorified in the salvation of

2. Carl Trueman, *The Rise and Triumph of the Modern Self: Cultural Amnesia, Expressive Individualism, and the Road to the Sexual Revolution* (Wheaton, Ill.: Crossway, 2020), 23.

3. David Ohana, *The Intellectual Origins of Modernity* (London: Routledge, 2019), 1.

sinners, we can and must bring the gospel winsomely and faithfully to the world around us. The outcome is in God's hands (1 Cor. 3:6–7), but He has commanded His church to make disciples of all nations. May we obediently and with love for others take up this vocation and see the fulfillment of our prayer that God's kingdom would come despite all opposition.

Questions for Reflection

1. How does recognizing that different sins often reinforce or build on one another help us diagnose and fight against them?

2. How can we benefit from Scripture's deconstruction or unveiling of the world's false claims regarding what it offers? What elements of our worldview require reinforcement so that Scripture's critiques of the world ring true for us?

3. How can Scripture's many promises about the sure outcome of God's purposes and the eternal security of His people encourage us when opposing forces seem to have the upper hand? How does understanding the already–not yet nature of the time between Christ's first and second comings help in this regard?

Resources

Johnson, Greg. *The World according to God: A Biblical View of Culture, Work, Science, Sex and Everything Else*. Downers Grove, Ill.: InterVarsity, 2002. 208 pp. A helpful, accessible analysis of the secular worldview and defense of a robust Christian worldview.

Piper, John. *Let the Nations Be Glad! The Supremacy of God in Missions*. 3rd edition. Grand Rapids: Baker Academic, 2010. 288 pp. A God-centered, practical explanation of Christian mission.

Platt, David. *Counter Culture: Following Christ in an Anti-Christian Age*. Carol Stream, Ill.: Tyndale Momentum, 2017. 320 pp. A clear, uncompromising treatment of Christian living in our secular world.

Rice, Tico, with Carl Laferton. *Honest Evangelism: How to Talk about Jesus Even When It's Tough*. Epsom: Good Book Company, 2015. 112 pp. A biblical, wise discussion of evangelism as a natural part of Christian living.

CHAPTER 5

Habakkuk and His Complaints

Habakkuk 1:1–2:1

The book of Habakkuk is unusual. In no other prophetic book does the prophet speak so regularly to God. Nor do other prophets typically protest with the vehemence of Habakkuk. Habakkuk is also unique because of the close connection of the book's message to the prophet's situation and concerns. Although these characteristics make the book rather curious, they also help the reader enter the understanding and experience of the prophet. As we will see, Habakkuk wrestles with an issue that is both common and difficult for believers to reckon with, and we can be thankful that his book presents his unvarnished struggle and subsequent transformation.

Historical Background

Although Habakkuk's first complaint concerns serious problems in Judah, Babylon receives much more attention as the means God will use to discipline His people. Like Assyria, Babylon boasted a long and illustrious history. By the beginning of the second millennium BC, Babylon was already prominent, and it expanded further under Hammurabi (ca. 1790–1750 BC), author of the law code that bears his name.[1] After several periods of relative weakness, Babylon again rose to power at the end of the second millennium but was gradually eclipsed by the neighboring state of Assyria. This led to a reasonably stable relationship between the two, with Babylon being a province with a special status in the Assyrian Empire, a status that sometimes meant having its own king (with or without Assyrian permission).[2] This situation continued for roughly two centuries before Babylon made a final attempt at independence in 652–648 BC. Assyria managed to quash the Babylonian desire for independence, but the effort proved too much. It was also poorly timed since Assyria grew weaker because of political instability from this point onward. By contrast, Babylon's star began to rise under Nabopolassar (626–605), who solidified Babylon's political independence from Assyria and began to attack Assyrian cities.[3]

From this point on, Babylon grew rapidly. With the help of the Medes, it conquered the Assyrian cities of Nineveh in 612 and Harran in about 610. Nabopolassar's son Nebuchadnezzar also drove the Egyptians out of the Levant at the battle of Carchemish in 605. Taking Assyria's place, as it were, Babylon soon brought Judah under its thumb and punished it for several attempts to reassert its independence before finally destroying

---

1. David S. Vanderhooft, "Babylonia and the Babylonians," in *The World around the Old Testament: The People and Places of the Ancient Near East*, ed. Bill T. Arnold and Brent A. Strawn (Grand Rapids: Baker Academic, 2016), 111.

2. Bill T. Arnold, *Who Were the Babylonians?*, Archaeology and Biblical Studies 10 (Atlanta: Society of Biblical Literature, 2004), 87–91, from which I draw occasionally in this paragraph.

3. Christopher B. Hays with Peter Machinist, "Assyria and the Assyrians," in *The World around the Old Testament: The People and Places of the Ancient Near East*, ed. Bill T. Arnold and Brent A. Strawn (Grand Rapids: Baker Academic, 2016), 56.

Jerusalem and deporting the king and the more skilled citizens of Judah in 586.

Much like Assyria, although with a bit less violence and bombast, Babylon too pursued its imperial project for theological and practical reasons. The god Marduk sat at the top of the Babylonian pantheon and was the theological source of Babylonian imperialism. Nabopolassar claimed that the god Marduk "called me to the lordship over the country and the people.... He let (me) succeed in everything I undertook. He caused Nergal, the strongest among the gods, to march at my side; he slew my foes, felled my enemies."[4]

Following his victory at Carchemish and the death of his father the same year, Nebuchadnezzar vigorously pursued the expansion of Babylon's control for the next decade.[5] In this he was successful, and by the 580s he had expanded the Babylonian Empire even beyond the size of the Assyrian Empire it had replaced.

Nebuchadnezzar also invested massive amounts of manpower and material in the reconstruction of Babylon. Like its imperialism, this effort was an explicitly theological project, focused on pleasing Marduk, and involved the expansion of Marduk's ziggurat and the temple complex that surrounded it in Babylon.[6] The king's piety was essential to the god-king

---

4. Paul-Alain Beaulieu, trans., "Nabopolassar's Restoration of Imgur-Enlil, the Inner Defensive Wall of Babylon (2.121)," *Context of Scripture*, volume 3, *Archival Documents from the Biblical World*, ed. W. W. Hallo and K. Lawson Younger Jr. (Leiden: Brill, 2003), 307.

5. D. J. Wiseman, "Babylonia 605–539 B.C.," in *Cambridge Ancient History*, vol. 3, part 2, ed. Boardman et al., 231, 236, whom I follow here.

6. Paul-Alain Beaulieu, "Mesopotamia," in *Religions of the Ancient World*, ed. S. I. Johnston (Cambridge, Mass.: Belknap Press, 2004), 171.

relationship. Like in Assyria, the chief god gave the king the right to rule the entire world. Nebuchadnezzar states that "Marduk… entrusted me with the rule of the totality of peoples, Nabu… placed in my hands a just scepter to lead all populated regions aright and to make humanity thrive."[7] Again, like their Assyrian predecessors, the Babylonian kings used the natural resources and manpower of those regions they conquered or controlled to embellish the empire and reinforce the empire's ideology. In Nebuchadnezzar's words,

> (All the widespread peoples), the governance of whom I exercise at the command of Marduk, my lord, and who carried mighty cedars from the mountain of Lebanon to Babylon, my city—all the peoples of the wide inhabited regions whom Marduk, my lord, bestowed upon me, I subjected them to corvée to build Etemenanki and I imposed the *tupšikku* [work basket] upon them.[8]

As we will see, this theologically founded imperialism is well known to Habakkuk and thus doubly objectionable, for it is simultaneously against God and against those who suffer at Babylon's hands.

Habakkuk's First Complaint and God's First Response

Habakkuk's book begins with an exasperated call for divine intervention: "O LORD, how long shall I cry?" (v. 2). These words capture one of the main themes of the book. On the one hand,

---

7. VAB 4 112, as quoted in David J. Vanderhooft, *The Neo-Babylonian Empire and Babylon in the Latter Prophets*, HSM 59 (Atlanta: Scholars, 1999), 35.

8. From the Nebuchadnezzar Cylinder IV, 1, trans. in David J. Vanderhooft, "'Nebuchadnezzar, King of Babylon, My Servant': Contrasting Prophetic Images of the Great King," *Hebrew Bible and Ancient Israel* 7 (2018): 95.

Habakkuk knows that only God can deliver him from the situation he finds unbearable. On the other hand, in Habakkuk's opinion, God should already have responded to his petition to act. This tension between what God's perfect wisdom has dictated and what Habakkuk considers best alerts the reader to the possibility that Habakkuk is losing his grasp on the theological convictions necessary to faithfulness in hard times. This is a potentially serious problem, and God does not overlook it or let Habakkuk persist in his misunderstanding. But even though the prophet's theology and attitude are heading off course, God deals very patiently and gently with him. This gentleness should characterize our efforts to help, encourage, and edify those who wrestle with similar situations and the questions they raise.

Lawlessness Is Rampant in Judah, yet God Seems Inactive

Habakkuk's first complaint in verses 2–4 expresses his outrage over widespread covenant infidelity among his compatriots in Judah. It is not too much to say that he considers the situation in Judah to be dire, if not beyond hope. He has observed in the daily lives of his fellow citizens, at least nominally God's people, a sobering number of grave sins. "Iniquity" and "plundering" and "violence" (v. 3) are all around him. Even though the king, the priests, and the prophets are supposed to teach, practice, and uphold God's law, Habakkuk realizes that the law itself is powerless to stop the offenders and that "strife and contention" (v. 3) are widespread in a society that is supposed to reflect the ideal of brotherly love (in Deut. 15:2, every Israelite is a "brother"), compassion and protection for the vulnerable (Deut. 14:29), and imitation of God's holiness (Lev. 19:2).[9]

The cumulative effect of these violations of the law's commands to love others as oneself (Lev. 19:18) is that justice, the very basis of social life (Gen. 18:19; Deut. 10:18; 16:18), is perverted. Far from pursuing obedience to God and practicing love and generosity, many Judeans in Habakkuk's day are simply ignoring God and His law, abusing whatever power they have to get ahead, and violating the trust and rights of their kin. The Judeans that Habakkuk regards with consternation are so committed to values and goals diametrically opposed to those set out in Scripture, and their social and religious power is so far-reaching, that only divine intervention can put a stop to this headlong plunge toward covenant rupture.

To make matters worse, Habakkuk sees God as part of the problem, so to speak. He asserts that God has not yet heard or saved as He should have ("O LORD, how long shall I cry, and You will not hear?" [1:2]) and is in some way responsible for the "iniquity" that He has caused Habakkuk to see, while God Himself looks at these wrongs but does not act ("Why do you show me iniquity, and cause me to see trouble?" [v. 3]). This leaves the prophet with no option but to voice his complaint to God, which he does in no uncertain terms. As we saw earlier, this puts the prophet in the risky position of criticizing God for the apparent tardiness of His justice. Yet Habakkuk's doubts are not without their limits. Even though he is dissatisfied with God's apparent

---

9. In the following sections I present some thoughts developed more fully in *The Theology of Nahum, Habakkuk, and Zephaniah*, Old Testament Theology (Cambridge: Cambridge University Press, forthcoming).

inactivity until now, his praying to God shows that he also trusts
that God will act justly and correct this lamentable situation.

God's First Response to Habakkuk

God's response to Habakkuk's prayer in verses 5–11 is not
what Habakkuk expected—and God knows this. God tells the
prophet in verse 5,

> Look among the nations and watch—
> Be utterly astounded!
> For I will work a work in your days
> Which you would not believe, though it were told you.

Yet this is more than simply the unexpected. The surprising
nature of what God is about to reveal to Habakkuk, like the
delay that led Habakkuk to complain in the first place and other
features I will note, are calculated to lead Habakkuk toward a
new understanding of God's justice. God does this either by
challenging what Habakkuk assumes to be normative (for example, the belief that God must deal with injustice without delay)
or by helping the prophet see that God's plans have already set
the course for justice (for example, Babylon's future punishment,
announced in chapter 2).

In this case, God announces that He will bring punishment on the Judah that Habakkuk knows is thoroughly guilty
by means of another guilty agent, the Babylonian Empire. God's
description of Babylon brings to the foreground the very elements that make His plan so shocking to Habakkuk, and this
seems to be intended to force Habakkuk to rethink how he eval-
uates God's justice. This "bitter and hasty" (v. 6) enemy is morally
flawed on numerous counts: it takes by force what belongs to
others, violating the eighth commandment. The Babylonians'

moral autonomy is evident in their conferring "their judgment and their dignity" on themselves (v. 7), without reference to any external norm, least of all God. The "violence" they commit (v. 9, the same term used in vv. 2–3 to describe the actions of some Judeans) makes them guilty of the same crimes as the Judeans Habakkuk condemns, albeit on a larger scale. God explicitly states that these transgressions make Babylon guilty ("commits offense," v. 11), and the last element mentioned is perhaps the worst: they ascribe their military might to their god. Whether this means that they simply attribute their military success to the involvement of their gods (which they surely did) or that they literally idolize that success (which was also quite likely), the overarching reality is that Babylon's imperial ideology involves the rejection of the true God in favor of a god of their own making.

Habakkuk's Second Complaint

God's first response to Habakkuk highlighted, rather than bypassed, several flagrant sins and moral flaws that were characteristic of the Babylonian Empire that God would use to punish His people. Whether Habakkuk perceived this strategy or not, he accepts God's description of Babylon but uses it as the basis of his second complaint (Hab. 1:12–2:1), protesting that God "cannot look on wickedness" (v. 13). In short, the prophet argues that God should not allow Babylon to continue acting in this way—above all against God's own people.

Habakkuk develops his argument carefully, beginning with a question: "Are You not from everlasting?" (v. 12). This is not a simple rhetorical question that affirms God's eternality. Instead, it implies that God, as the Creator of all things who has ruled over them from the beginning, can and should exercise His rule over all things, *but on Habakkuk's terms*. The tension we noted in the book's opening words is present here as well. Although the prophet recognizes that God has "appointed" Babylon as the means He will use to judge and correct His people (v. 12), he finds this divine decision questionable. Asserting rightly that God is not indifferent before evil, Habakkuk then asks God why He allows the wicked to "devour" those who are more righteous than they are (v. 13). To drive this point home, the prophet argues that God is not caring as He ought for those whom Babylon conquers or kills: "Why do You make men like fish of the sea, like creeping things that have no rule over them?" (v. 14). Continuing his comparison of the empire's victims to fish, Habakkuk contends (with good reason) that Babylon uses every means at its disposal to dominate the surrounding nations and is satisfied with its success: "They rejoice and are glad" (v. 15).

To this he adds the Babylonians' idolatry (mentioned in v. 11) and draws attention to the excessive appetite for the spoils of war and the enslavement of conquered peoples. An extract from Nebuchadnezzar's royal annals shows how closely interwoven the empire's material riches and its worship of its gods were in the empire's thinking: "Gold, silver, exceedingly valuable gemstones, thick cedars, heavy tribute, expensive presents, the produce of all countries, goods from all inhabited regions, before Marduk the great lord, the god who created me, and Nabû his lofty heir who loves my kingship, I transported and brought into Esagil and Ezida."[10]

---

10. As quoted in Vanderhooft, *Neo-Babylonian Empire*, 46.

This final charge of idolatry is probably the most serious offense of all those listed, as the order of the Ten Commandments suggests. This gives the greatest possible force to the prophet's final question—whether God will allow this reprehensible abuse of power and idolatry to go unchecked: "Shall they therefore empty their net, and continue to slay nations without pity?" (v. 17). If the prophet were to answer his own question, the answer would be "surely not," to which he would add that God's intervention will follow *without delay*.

Before we continue, we need to be sure that we have not misjudged the prophet by suggesting that the content of his complaint, if not its tone, is flawed. In favor of vindicating the prophet, we could argue that God does not rebuke him as He did Job, whose accusations were sometimes unqualified and blunt (see Job 38:2; 40:2). Yet there is something inherently troubling in Habakkuk's impassioned argument that God has *wrongly* remained inactive in the face of sin. If God were to punish all sin immediately, even with merely temporal consequences, who would survive? No less importantly, this desire to see even partial justice done without delay militates against God's characteristic patience with sinners as He calls them to repent lest judgment come on them (Ezek. 18:23, 31–32; 33:11; Amos 5:4, 6, 14).

This weakness in Habakkuk's contention with God is not all that should be said about it, however. The last words of the prophet's second complaint give us valuable insight into his belief that God will answer him, although the answer may not come right away. Further, he will carefully consider how he should respond "when I am corrected" (2:1), a phrase that might also be translated "concerning my complaint" (ESV). Since God's second response does not reprove Habakkuk for any particular flaw (at least not explicitly), it seems more likely that the prophet does not expect a certain type of response (that is, correction), but does expect that God's reply will address the concerns and apparent problems that he raised in his second complaint.

Habakkuk's attitude is thus one of openness to what God will say. Despite his unanswered questions, the prophet is not ready to condemn God's apparent inaction in the face of evil. The clearest proof of this is Habakkuk's regular use of questions rather than statements when he refers to the apparent divine inactivity or laxness that he has trouble understanding. Thus, he asks God, "How long?" (1:2); "Why?" (1:3, 13); "Are You not?" (1:12); and "Shall they?" (1:17). This kind of exchange with God in prayer meets with divine approval in the case of Abraham, who asks (with the intention of moving God to act in a certain way) whether God will destroy "the righteous with the wicked" (Gen. 18:23). Like Habakkuk, Abraham asserts that God is righteous (v. 25) even as he requests that God act in keeping with his own understanding of these things. We may well be puzzled by God's providence, and such confusion naturally gives rise to questions like Abraham's and Habakkuk's. At the same time, precisely because we are puzzled but do not have even a fraction of the knowledge necessary to exhaustively evaluate the situation in question, we have no grounds for charging God with injustice.

J. I. Packer gives sound advice for how believers should face trials like these. "How are we to meet these baffling and trying situations, if we cannot for the moment see God's purpose in them? First, by taking them as from God, and asking ourselves what reactions to them, and in them, the gospel of God requires

of us; second, by seeking God's face specifically about them."[11]
Even at this relatively early stage of his conversation with God,
Habakkuk is convinced that the current evil in Judah and the
coming Babylonian attack are from God, having come about
with His permission and as part of His wise and good plan for
His people. As the book itself shows, he ardently seeks God's
face to understand these puzzling situations. But he is not yet at
a point where, to rephrase Packer's advice, he asks himself what
kinds of reactions to them he should have considering God's
character and purposes. That will change drastically once he has
heard and believed God's second response.

Questions for Reflection

1. Discuss or contemplate the importance of remaining cor-
   rigible and humble in our struggles to understand God's
   mysterious ways in our lives.

2. Discuss or contemplate the value and propriety of wrestling
   with mysterious providences in prayer and meditation
   on Scripture.

3. How does Asaph qualify and ultimately contradict some of
   his impressions or conclusions earlier in Psalm 73? How does
   Psalm 73:15–17 describe his response to his earlier thinking?

4. Reflect on the importance of God's word for Habakkuk
   throughout the book as he wrestles with difficult situations
   that affect him directly. Why do our feelings or the opinions

---

11. J. I. Packer, *Knowing God* (Downers Grove, Ill.: InterVarsity, 1973), 98.

of others sometimes take priority over what God says in His word? How can we avoid this error? "As Satan then disturbs us in various ways, the Prophet shows that the word of God alone is sufficient for us."[12]

Resources

Boston, Thomas. *The Crook in the Lot: What to Believe When Our Lot in Life Is Not Health, Wealth, and Happiness.* Puritan Paperbacks. Edinburgh: Banner of Truth Trust, 2017. 168 pp. A classic treatment of Christian suffering.

Carson, D. A. *How Long, O Lord? Reflections on Suffering and Evil.* 2nd ed. Grand Rapids: Baker Academic, 2006. 240 pp. An excellent exploration of evil and suffering.

Packer, J. I. *Knowing God.* Downers Grove, Ill.: IVP, 1973. 287 pp. A stellar and practical treatment of God's attributes and more. See especially chapter 9 ("God Only Wise") for an excellent, brief discussion of suffering and how to glorify God in it.

---

12. John Calvin, *Commentaries on the Twelve Minor Prophets*, vol. 4, *Habakkuk, Zephaniah, Haggai*, trans. J. Owen (Grand Rapids: Baker, 2003), 62.

CHAPTER 6

God's Response:
I Will Eliminate Evil
Habakkuk 2:2–20

Unlike Job, Habakkuk will receive in response to his prayer a divine reply that clearly sketches God's purposes in allowing Babylon to serve as the means for His punishment of Judah. The prophet already knows that God will use Babylon to punish Judah (Hab. 1:12) but is bewildered by a just God's use of an instrument that in Habakkuk's opinion is worse than the Judeans He will punish. God does not directly address the prophet's opinion, and God's second response focuses mainly on His certain punishment of Babylon for its many wrongs committed in relation to its imperialism and violence toward other nations.

The Lesser or Greater Righteousness of Judah and Babylon

But God using Babylon to punish Judah without any hint of injustice or self-incrimination leads us to conclude that either such scenarios are permissible, or Babylon is not demonstrably worse than Judah. Both possibilities may be true and valid. God alone can evaluate the guilt of a group such as Babylon or Judah, and while Babylon's larger size and greater power entailed a proportionally larger degree of responsibility, Judah too was privileged in ways that also involve great responsibility, being the only one of "all the families of the earth" that God has "known" and chosen for Himself (Amos 3:2). The inestimable privileges of adoption, glory, the covenants and the law, worship of God, and the promises conferred on Israel make for such a great degree of responsibility that it is hard to conclude it was less guilty than Babylon.

Be that as it may, God's actions, as well as the absence of any rebuttal of Habakkuk's implicit accusation that a less guilty party cannot be punished justly by means of a more guilty party, seem to dismiss that element of the prophet's argument. Here the limits of human knowledge play an important role in how we respond to these situations. In light of God's greatness, infinity, and omniscience, it is inevitable that we will never fully know or understand His purposes. Yet we do know with certitude that He is just, holy, and trustworthy, and so we can trust Him to do what is best to resolve problems that we cannot fully understand.

The Heart of the Matter

Before God speaks about the role of Babylon in His plan for His people, He reassures the prophet in Habakkuk 2:2–5 that what He is about to say will come to pass, *even if the prophet must wait for that to come about.* This addresses one of Habakkuk's concerns expressed in the "How long?" that begins his first complaint. Whereas the prophet fails to see the wisdom of God's timing in punishing sin in Judah and Babylon because in both cases he thinks it is delayed or tardy, God asserts that He has "an appointed time" (v. 3) at which He will establish justice (cf. "proper time" in Ps. 75:2). Habakkuk is probably the messenger charged with conveying God's message to Judah and is to tell others—and believe himself—what God insists on here:

> For the vision is yet for an appointed time;
> But at the end it will speak, and it will not lie.

Though it tarries, wait for it;
Because it will surely come,
It will not tarry. (Hab. 2:3)

There is a time fixed by God when the vision of Babylon's fall will be fulfilled. The vision is not a lie but will surely come to pass, and even if it should seem to be delayed, Habakkuk must wait patiently for it to be fulfilled, for it will surely happen.

For God's word to have the intended effect, it must be received with faith. God puts this in very blunt terms, stating that only two responses are possible. Either a person's arrogant heart will lead him into what is not upright, or the just person will "live by his faith" (Hab. 2:4). Keeping in mind the parallelism that characterizes Hebrew poetry, note that this short verse makes several important points that contrast these radically different responses to Yahweh's word.

Defining Characteristic	Pride	Faith
Status	Not upright	Just
Outcome	(Implicit: die)	Live

The contrasts in the table above are meant to convince the reader of the wisdom of trusting God. Not to trust Him involves unreasonable pride, whereas faith is inseparable from a humility that recognizes the need for God's grace and the inability to deliver oneself. The status of the person concerned follows inevitably on his or her attitude before God. Only by trusting in God's promises to deliver, even in their nascent form as expressed in Habakkuk, can a person obtain a righteousness that will deliver from God's judgment. Contrariwise, those who would make themselves the masters of their destiny cut off access to the only possible escape from the moral and spiritual dilemma that they fail almost completely to understand (Rom. 1:17).

There is thus a terrible irony in people proudly seeking to control their own life to get what they want out of it. Even if, like Babylon, a person can control, benefit from, use, and abuse an almost unlimited number of people, resources, and events, God has determined that such a lifestyle produces death. And what better way to resolve Habakkuk's doubts than to show that this is the case with Babylon? The last lines of Habakkuk 2:5, in which the "proud" person takes on the traits of an empire that gathers for itself "all nations" and "heaps up for himself all peoples," lead directly into the second part of Yahweh's response, which will answer Habakkuk's questions once and for all.

Babylon's Proud Attempt to Rule
God's World Punished and Undone

Babylon, an empire that proudly pursued domination on a large scale while attributing its success to its gods and treating those weaker than itself as it saw fit, embodies the human predicament. The corrupt nature with which every human being other than Jesus Christ has been born is profoundly egocentric. Regardless of the ways that each person expresses this, it involves giving pride of place to our desires and our values. In God's common grace, the effects of this disposition on others are relatively limited if we compare them to the depiction of Babylon here. But its self-focused nature is the same. In keeping with the summary statement about faith in verse 4, the rest of chapter 2 (vv. 6–20) contrasts the arrogant empire that is obsessed with its self-serving projects with a perspective in which the living God is sovereign, active, and unstoppable. The posture of heart that Habakkuk and his audience should have is trust in God's power and goodness and faith in His promise that He will destroy not only Babylon but all evil, in whatever form it exists, and establish His kingdom across the globe:

> The earth will be filled
> With the knowledge of the glory of the LORD,
> As the waters cover the sea. (v. 14)

God's promise to destroy Babylon and all opposition to His saving purposes for His people takes the form of five announcements of woe. Each woe identifies one or more actions that render Babylon guilty, then spells out the punishment that will follow (only hinted at in vv. 18–20). God, speaking through Habakkuk, condemns the Babylonian Empire, and specifically its king (referred to as "him" in verse 6), for a wide variety of military, diplomatic, and religious activities, most of which were already mentioned in Habakkuk 1. The first woe (vv. 6–8) predicts that many nations, including those whom Babylon has violently mistreated, robbed, and plundered, will plunder it: "Because you have plundered many nations, all the remnant of the people shall plunder you" (v. 8). Its massive material wealth will be of no avail to Babylon when Yahweh's punishment falls on it.

In the second woe (vv. 9–11), God promises that Babylon's attempt to provide absolute security for itself will come to nothing and that its violent self-aggrandizement will ironically lead to its shame and death (v. 10). Then, as now, if a person ignores the reality of life after death and a final judgment, he or she can imagine that a life sweetened by material wealth and ease will satisfy. This naive belief is disproven a thousand times over every day, as the average wealth of people especially in the West continues to rise and their overall sense of well-being and content continues to decline. Furthermore, no less today than in the seventh century BC, God's judgment cannot be avoided, regardless of how many assets and accomplishments people may have to their credit. Death is the great leveler, and only God can deliver from it (Ps. 49:15–20). In the case of Babylon, there will be no escape.

The third woe (Hab. 2:12–14) condemns Babylon's violence yet again and foretells that Babylon's massive building projects and infrastructure, built primarily by the people it conquered and conscripted, will come to nothing. Whatever dividends sin seems to pay, they will be lost sooner or later, to the bitter disappointment of the sinner. The repeated condemnation of violence in these woes ("blood…violence," v. 8; "bloodshed… iniquity," v. 12; "violence…blood…violence," v. 17) is a very clear reminder that human life belongs to God and that it should only be taken by human hands when justice demands it (Gen. 9:6; Rom. 13:1–5). Every human being, regardless of the individual's gifts, limits, or capacities, is made in God's image and, as such, is to be accorded dignity appropriate to his or her worth. Babylon's cold-blooded violence against entire groups and nations, treating them like the fish that a fisherman normally and acceptably catches and kills, thus militates against the very nature of its victims and against the God who has created them in His image.

The last line of Habakkuk 2:14 stands out for its exceptional power and significance. The promise that knowledge of God's glory will cover the earth reveals that much more is at issue in these woes and in God's answer to Habakkuk than the fall of the Babylonian Empire. A world in which all know the glory of Yahweh is a world in which He receives the honor and worship that is His due, in which His justice has brought an end to all sin, and in which all find in Him life and holistic well-being.

Contrast this sure vision of the future with Babylon's exceedingly tenuous imperial project. Babylon's elite pursue their own glory and share it with the gods they have created in their own image. Babylon's violence in particular results in its dealing out death to those who will not fall under its sway, mimicking in a terribly perverted way God's unique claim to sovereignty over human beings and their fate. Babylon's "judgment," or justice, is its own (Hab. 1:7) and so can be only a chimera, a false moral norm that authorizes its self-serving and God-defying behavior. Finally, the so-called deliverance that Babylon brings is defined as serving the empire, whether by constraint or freely, and thus serving a kingdom of merely human origin. As such, Babylon exhibits on a large scale all the typical signs of human weaknesses and corruption. Far from being able to save others or itself, it brings about its own destruction by pursuing its own salvation on its own terms.

Babylon is thus a perfect prototype of contemporary secular culture, in which individuals are accorded absolute freedom to define who and what they are and what is right and wrong. Salvation, insofar as it exists conceptually, is purely imminent and consists in self-realization—people becoming who they want to be—and is therefore profoundly egocentric, individualistic, and secular. As sad as this reality is, and as surely as it should be critiqued and questioned with honesty and rigor, it should also be exposed so that those who hold to it might see its destructive power.

It is self-evident that a worldview focused on *my* realization of *my* ideals above all else is incompatible with any human society, regardless of its political form. Further, behind the facade of contentment and significance that depend on *my* attaining *my* self-determined identity and happiness lies the inevitable danger of failure. Who can give themselves the significance, value, and meaning necessary to bear up under the difficulties of life as a fallen human being in a world subjected to the effects of sin (Rom. 8:19–22)? Many people around us are aware, to one degree or another, that this kind of worldview cannot bring happiness, contentment, or meaning, nor can it offer hope to those who have tried and failed to attain those goals.

The gospel cuts through the false hopes, naively optimistic humanism, and fragile secularism of modernity and holds out the uniquely solid ground of creation by God and in His image; the reality of sin and corruption that explains us and our world; and the possibility of real, holistic salvation that does not depend on our strength, resilience, or self-conferred goodness. This is the gospel that we need to share with those around us and embody in our lives and attitudes.

In the fourth woe (Hab. 2:15–17), God condemns the deceitful and exploitative nature of Babylon's diplomacy and interaction with other nations. The metaphor is one of sexual abuse, with the schemes and deceit of the empire leading its unsuspecting and vulnerable victim to put himself in a position to be exploited and abused:

> Woe to him who gives drink to his neighbor,
> Pressing him to your bottle,
> Even to make him drunk,
> That you may look on his nakedness! (v. 15).

The fault clearly lies with the abuser, who has gained the trust of his victim and who is motivated by a lust that must be satisfied by any means necessary. Here again the violation of creational norms underlies Habakkuk's condemnation.

The nakedness that is metaphorically exposed is a corruption of the nonthreatening, healthy openness and safety that are at the heart of the marriage relationship (Gen. 2:25). The metaphor thus targets Babylon's illegitimate use of others for its own corrupt purposes and the pride and sense of entitlement that involves. Added to this pattern of grave violations of justice and right on the international scene is Babylon's destructive misuse of natural resources from Lebanon in particular. These resources are used without any recognition that they belong first to God as their Creator (Pss. 50:10–11; 104:16–18). All this portrays Babylon as attempting to usurp God's role and glory in every way possible. With the irony that always attends sin's punishment, God will punish this headlong pursuit of glory and permanence with shame and destruction.

The final woe (Hab. 2:18–20) condemns Babylon's idolatry, which played a key role in the empire's decision-making and military activity. This is the heart of Babylon's sin, as it was the root sin of the characteristically proud person in verse 4. In creating gods in its own image and trusting in them, Babylon effectively trusts in its own power, stratagems, and knowledge. It is, in short, its own god, and it attempts to do all that it does as if the Lord did not exist. While verse 14 has already announced that Babylon and all who reject God's claims on them as Creator will vanish, verse 20 intimates that this will involve catastrophic judgment and so calls for all on earth to "keep silence before Him." God will not share His glory with anyone or anything (Isa. 48:11).

Questions for Reflection

1. How does the spiritual and moral critique of Babylon prevent us from interpreting God's judgment as focused on a particular nation considered as a political unit? How does it compare with Habakkuk's description of Judah in Habakkuk 1:2–4?

2. Taking our cue from Revelation's use of Babylon to refer to the ideology, violence, oppression, and pride of the Roman Empire (17:1–19:5), how should we understand Habakkuk's prophecy today? Where, in the world or in the church, do you see idolatry, abuse of power, trust in human means, and self-determination or autonomy?

3. How does faith in God's promise enable believers to wait for His intervention in His time rather than according to our personal timetable? How should this waiting period develop and strengthen our faith?

4. How should God's promise that He will ultimately destroy all evil affect the way we read the news, think about our world, interact with non-Christians, and evangelize? How is the resurrection of Jesus Christ a down payment on the fulfillment of this promise?

Resources

Smith, James K. *How (Not) to Be Secular: Reading Charles Taylor*. Grand Rapids: Eerdmans, 2014. 160 pp. A very accessible guide to and summary of Taylor's book.

Taylor, Charles. *A Secular Age*. Cambridge, Mass.: Belknap, 2007. 896 pp. An exhaustive analysis of how the contemporary secular world came to be.

Trueman, Carl R. *The Rise and Triumph of the Modern Self: Cultural Amnesia, Expressive Individualism, and the Road to the Sexual Revolution*. Wheaton, Ill.: Crossway, 2020. 432 pp. A probing analysis of how recent social ideologies and imaginaries have established themselves in Western culture.

CHAPTER 7

Trusting God through Bad Times
Habakkuk 3

The final chapter of Habakkuk reveals that the prophet has been radically affected by God's promise to punish Babylon and ultimately to establish His just kingdom and spread His glory across the world. This reorientation is the result of a radical change in the way that the prophet interprets reality. None of the data on which he based his earlier arguments have changed: Judah continues mired in injustice, Babylon remains as powerful and godless as it was, and God still has not punished Babylon. What has changed, however, is the prophet's understanding of God's justice, wisdom, and goodness.

In chapter 3, Habakkuk's questions give way to assertions of faith based on his corrected and deepened knowledge of God. The prophet was hardly lukewarm or unorthodox before this change, but his conclusion that God had not implemented His justice at the right time or to the right degree has now been corrected by what Habakkuk has learned of God's character and purposes. The theology of the book of Habakkuk is thus very literally practical, meaning effective and transformative, in the life of the prophet as it should be in ours.

Reorientation

Compared to the persistent questions in Habakkuk's first two responses, the prayer of chapter 3 is quite different. In terms of tone, there is no longer any doubt or critique of what God is doing or will soon do, proof that Habakkuk is now fully convinced that God can be just even if divine justice is not exercised immediately. In terms of content, the prophet's restored confidence in divine justice makes him acutely aware of the need for mercy. Submission to God's sovereignty and unqualified trust in God's wisdom, justice, and goodness enable Habakkuk to face grave difficulties with confidence and humility. In short, he trusts that God will orchestrate all things for the good of His people and the glory of His name even if Habakkuk cannot fully understand how this is so.

Verse 2 of this chapter brings these points together in a powerful way before the prophet moves on to a meditation on God's past interventions in history:

> O LORD, I have heard Your speech and was afraid;
> O LORD, revive Your work in the midst of the years!
> In the midst of the years make it known;
> In wrath remember mercy.

With the prophecies of Babylon's judgment in chapter 2 fresh in mind, and against the more immediate background of the punishment looming over Judah, Habakkuk reckons with the necessity and certainty of Yahweh's acts in both contexts. The radically different roles of Judah as God's people and Babylon as their enemy produce very different reactions on the part of the prophet. On the one hand, he truly desires God to continue His work, while on the other hand, he asks God to temper His wrath with His mercy. Even if we assume that Habakkuk requests mercy for Judah and not for Babylon, he surely does not mean for God to overlook sin and its punishment. Nor does he imply that all in Judah will suffer the punishment of violence and exile at Babylon's hands for the same reason or to the same degree. Rather, he prays that God would show His displeasure with Judah "in such a way as to afford to the faithful at the same time some taste of his favour and mercy by finding him to be propitious to them."[1] These attitudes, formed by God's reaffirmation of His commitment to justice with respect to Babylon, are further developed in light of Habakkuk's meditation on God's past actions in behalf of His people and in defense of His name. This meditation sets the Judah-Babylon scenario in a larger context of past and future divine intervention in which God as divine warrior destroys His enemies and establishes His justice once and for all. The cross and the second coming of our Lord Jesus Christ are the culmination of this trajectory, bringing full salvation to God's people and final destruction to His enemies.

Past and Future in the Present

The verb in the first line of Habakkuk's meditation in Habakkuk 3:3, "God came from Teman" (an imperfective form), suggests that at least some of what follows is the anticipation of future acts of divine justice and deliverance rather than a simple meditation on the past. There are, however, clear echoes of several remarkable episodes in Israel's history when God's power was clearly exercised, including the exodus (vv. 3, 5) the theophany at Sinai (v. 4), and the conquest of Canaan (v. 11). Habakkuk's

---

1. John Calvin, *Habakkuk, Zephaniah, Haggai*, vol. 4 of *Commentaries on the Twelve Minor Prophets*, trans. J. Owen, in vol. 15 of *Calvin's Commentaries* (Grand Rapids: Baker Books, 2003), 139.

meditation thus has something in common with the use of the sacraments, in which God declares and seals to us "the promise of the gospel" (Heidelberg Catechism 66).

God's past liberation of Israel from bondage in Egypt, His provision for them during decades in the wilderness, and many more acts of blessing and deliverance become grounds for Habakkuk to reaffirm and strengthen his trust in God's commitment to punish Judah in a way that upholds His justice and His mercy. Similarly, God's decimation of the Egyptians, who rejected His sovereign claims over His people, and His routing of Israel's enemies, so that they could possess the land of Canaan, demonstrate His resolute justice and power against those who refuse to bend the knee before Him.

Habakkuk's faith-driven reflection on the past as proof that God will not merely continue but will consummate His work of salvation and judgment also includes a shift from the narrow focus of Judah and Babylon to a wider—indeed, global—perspective (recall the global scope of Hab. 2:14). Whereas Babylon and Judah were very clearly the subjects in chapters 1 and 2, they are not mentioned in the psalm of chapter 3. In their place are two groups who are less easily identified, God's people (v. 13, including His "Anointed") on one side, and "the nations" (vv. 6, 12) or "the wicked" (v. 13) on the other (only two groups or territories are mentioned, Cushan and Midian, in v. 7).

This shift in focus from particular nations to more general categories may seem insignificant, but it is necessary because what Habakkuk anticipates in chapter 3 is nothing less than the full elimination of evil. Yes, God has promised to deal with Babylon, but that temporal and limited judgment of evil is inseparable from God's final, definitive punishment of sin and

sinners and His deliverance of those who receive His justice by
faith. God's purposes reach all the way to the new heavens and
the new earth, to a world purified of sin and in which "righteousness dwells" (2 Peter 3:13).

The way to this final goal is twofold. First, it involves judgment against all those (Israelite or not) who, as the "nations"
typically did in the Old Testament, resist God's rule and will
rather than repenting (Hab. 3:12–14). It also involves God's
unmerited deliverance of His people not only or primarily from
their earthly enemies but from their sin and the punishment it
demands (v. 13). Israel's sacrificial system had borne witness to
this reality since the nation was constituted at Sinai, so God's
promise to fully deliver His faithful people from all their enemies necessarily includes the full atonement for their sins (note
how Romans 1 places salvation [vv. 16–17] and judgment
[vv. 18–32] side by side). Habakkuk is not given a full explanation of either facet of God's future work, whether the destruction
of evil or the provision of full atonement and righteousness for
His people. Nonetheless, the prophet unhesitatingly places his
faith in these promises and in the faithful God who made them.

The New Testament teaches that Jesus Christ has accomplished, by His perfect obedience and His substitutionary death,
the righteousness that God requires and has atoned for the sins of
His people (Rom. 5:12–21; 2 Cor. 5:21; 1 Peter 2:21–25). This
is the most solid ground possible on which to base our trust in
God's goodness and justice, even in the face of the greatest challenges imaginable. If God has orchestrated and brought about
such a marvelous plan of salvation, of which we are the undeserv-
ing beneficiaries, how can we doubt that He will maintain His
justice in every situation of our lives? Like Habakkuk, we may

have to wait a long time or may never even see the resolution of a particular problem in this life. But we are assured by God's Word and His countless demonstrations of His justice in history and in our lives that He *will* act justly and that His actions *will* bring about His good and just purposes (Rev. 16:5–7).

This meditation on God's demonstrated justice and mercy in Jesus Christ brings us back to Habakkuk's response. Although by virtue of what God has done in Christ and the fuller revelation that presents and interprets that for us in the New Testament, we still do not yet see the final fulfillment of these things. Perhaps the hardest part of dealing with unresolved suffering or injustice is leaving it in God's hands, trusting Him when we do not (and cannot) fully understand His purposes in every detail. This was no impediment to Habakkuk's rekindled faith. The prophet is not blind to the challenges of faith in the face of hardship and even judgment. On the contrary, he is overwhelmed by his understanding of what God will do. His "body trembled," his "lips quivered," and "rottenness entered [his] bones" (Hab. 3:16); and he realizes that life before the experience of deliverance will be very difficult. But all of this is overcome by his trust in God as *his* salvation, and this trust produces joy amid suffering!

> Though the fig tree may not blossom,
> Nor fruit be on the vines;
> Though the labor of the olive may fail,
> And the fields yield no food;
> Though the flock may be cut off from the fold,
> And there be no herd in the stalls—
> Yet I will rejoice in the LORD,
> I will joy in the God of my salvation. (vv. 17–18)

The strength needed to traverse this period of extreme difficulty is found in God alone, who will preserve him and ultimately welcome him into a world in which all know Yahweh's saving goodness:

> The LORD God is my strength;
> He will make my feet like deer's feet,
> And He will make me walk on my high hills. (v. 19)

Questions for Reflection

1. How do the sacraments remind us of what God has done in the past?

2. How can the typological relationships between Christ's work as represented in the sacraments and what God has done in the Old Testament help us nourish our faith and knowledge of God based on the exodus, Israel's entry into Canaan and eventual possession of the land, and other events to which Habakkuk 3 alludes?

3. How does the truth that God is the same yesterday, today, and forever help us trace His work from the past, through our present, and into the future until Christ's return? How should God's faithful, unchanging, just, and compassionate character affect our attitudes and outlook?

4. Contrast Habakkuk's attitude in Habakkuk 3 with his initial
   questioning of God in chapter 1. State in your own words
   how the content of the book explains that change, then restate
   that with respect to your own life, considering the gospel: "I
   confess, Lord, that I do not understand why _____.
   Despite my lack of understanding, I know that I can trust
   Your wisdom, grace, power, and goodness as You have fully
   revealed them to me in Jesus Christ. Grant me the grace
   to remain calm, trusting, and obedient as I wait for You to
   intervene in this situation, in your time."

Resources

Thomas, Heath A. *Faith amid the Ruins: The Book of Habakkuk*.
       Bellingham, Wash.: Lexham, 2016. 112 pp. A helpful
       guide to the theology and message of Habakkuk.

CHAPTER 8

From Creation to Sin and Judgment

Zephaniah 1:2–3, 14–18

The book of Zephaniah could well be subtitled *Paradise Lost, Paradise Regained*. Although the messages of Nahum and Habakkuk occasionally dealt with the world, their primary focus was mostly particular nations. This focus also meant that relatively little attention was given to Judah, especially in the case of Nahum. Zephaniah's book is quite different and gives roughly equal attention to Judah and to individual nations. The book's perspective is therefore universal from start to finish, and the different scenes and announcements that the prophet presents capture God's multifaceted dealings with humanity from creation to the new heavens and the new earth. And all in three chapters!

Like the other books we have studied, Zephaniah uses a wide array of literary skills and rhetoric as he communicates God's word to Judah. He presents images of judgment as if no escape were possible, calls for repentance without guaranteeing that it will deliver his audience from judgment, and uses bold, dark colors in his depictions of divine judgment. Yet his book also includes brilliant descriptions of divine mercy and deliverance and sublime depictions of God's restored, perfected relationship with His people as He forgives their sin and creates a new world without sin. The message of Zephaniah, then, is nothing less than the gospel prophesied.

Historical Background

The religious, political, and social realities in Judah near the end of the seventh century BC are very prominent in Zephaniah. The prophet's genealogy ties him to the royal family, and his familiarity with details of life in the royal court (see Zeph. 1:8) and in Jerusalem (see 1:10–12) point to someone very familiar with life in Jerusalem. This firsthand knowledge of social and religious practices in Jerusalem is almost entirely negative, however, and raises the question whether Zephaniah ministered before, during, or after the reforms that Josiah implemented beginning in his eighth year (ca. 632 BC; 2 Chron. 34:3–7) and pursued in earnest once the book of the law (almost certainly Deuteronomy) was found in about 622 (2 Kings 23:25).

The long reign of Josiah's grandfather Manasseh (698–642) had inflicted massive damage on the practice of orthodox worship and belief in Judah. In addition to restoring the illicit worship sites that Hezekiah had destroyed, Manasseh built altars to gods such as Baal in the temple and elsewhere (2 Kings 21:3–6). He also practiced divination, most likely as an effort to make savvy diplomatic and political decisions, rather than seeking God's will or following His word. Sadly, many of the people followed the king rather than God and became more sinful than the nations around them. This collective apostasy made exile inevitable (vv. 9–15).

It is this situation that preoccupies Zephaniah, perhaps even more than events on the international scene. Beyond Judah's borders, other sources reveal that the decline of Assyria had begun, although there would have been little reason to think it would disappear from the scene in the near future. Indeed, its pride and insouciance, as described in the oracle against it (Zeph. 2:13–15), suggest that from Judah's perspective, it was still an important figure on the international scene. This, together with the absence of Babylon from Zephaniah, implies that the prophet's ministry was earlier rather than later in Josiah's reign and either helped begin or encouraged Josiah's reforms (or both). Aggression by the states around Judah, including Moab and Ammon, as well as key Philistine cities (vv. 4–10), occurred occasionally (2 Kings 3; 13:20; 24:2; 2 Chronicles 20), and insofar as Assyrian control over them loosened during Josiah's reign, aggression against Judah would have been more likely as they tried to compensate for the decline of their former protector.

From Creation to Sin and Judgment

The first words of Zephaniah's message (1:2–3) are incredibly powerful and somber. God Himself announces that He will "utterly consume everything from the face of the land," even the fish and the birds! It is easy to recognize echoes of the biblical account of the flood (see Gen. 6:7, 13; 7:21–23; 8:21) and to assume that God announces judgment here for the same reason. But before we look at the condemnations and announcements of judgment in this chapter, we need to step back in time all the way to creation if we are to understand the gravity of this judgment. The flood had come long before Zephaniah announced his message of imminent destruction and was not to be repeated (Gen. 8:21). To understand the terrifying message of Zephaniah 1, we first need to understand the gravity of sin that evokes it, and that requires us to consider the world as God made it, before sin and "very good."[1]

---

1. In the following sections, I present in brief some thoughts I develop more

The Biblical Creation Accounts

The twin accounts of creation in Genesis 1:1–2:3 and 2:4–24 present complementary records of God's act of creation. The first creation account includes crucially important affirmations, the first of which is the creature/Creator distinction. God exists prior to and independently of all things, and the created order is entirely dependent on His will for its existence. Second, considering the rest of Scripture, we can discern the Trinitarian nature of God's creative work, in which God's word and Spirit are active and effective (see for example John 1:3; Col. 1:16). Third, the structure of Genesis 1, with the frequent repetition of divine speech, the reality that it creates, and the closure of that day, emphasizes the order of God's work and the absence of any other causes for what He brings into existence. Fourth, God's creation as far as it had progressed by the third day is "good," and the account of the sixth day asserts first that it is "good" and then "very good" once Adam and Eve have been created as the pinnacle of the divine work of creation (note the "not good" status of Adam being alone in Gen. 2:18).

Created sinless, the first couple began their lives as God's image-bearers in fellowship with Him and in humble, trusting obedience to His commands. This magnificent picture is rounded out by the larger context of a world and a cosmos in which all things, animate and inanimate, fulfill the functions and roles for which God had created them. In a word, God's entire creation is, in ways appropriate to each element of it, in a harmonious relationship with Him that glorifies Him. This happy scenario also brings good to the creation and especially to

---

fully in *The Theology of Nahum, Habakkuk, and Zephaniah*, Old Testament Theology (Cambridge: Cambridge University Press, forthcoming).

obedient humanity as it awaits the consummation prefigured in the divine rest of the seventh day.

The second creation narrative focuses more narrowly on the first couple. Most of Genesis 2 describes how God provided all that was necessary for Adam, creating and bringing to him Eve as his complement and companion. God also provides for the first couple, creating a garden that contained all that was necessary for their life and flourishing. Within this account we find both the vocation given to Adam and Eve to work and keep the garden and a single, profoundly important element of prohibition (vv. 16–17). Amid all the bounty and beauty of the garden, God forbids access to one tree associated with the "knowledge of good and evil" (v. 17), threatening disobedience of that command with death.

As Genesis 3 shows, this prohibition serves as a means for the first couple to demonstrate their trust in God's goodness and wisdom rather than follow the temptation to proudly distrust Him and attempt to live independently of Him. In a tragedy that exceeds all understanding, Adam and Eve chose to follow their will rather than God's and so brought sin and death into the world. This same sin, present in all born from them, quickly grows to a horrific extent and leads God to announce that judgment must follow (Genesis 6).

Judgment of Sin as the Undoing of Creation and Humanity in Zephaniah

This brief glance at Genesis enables us to understand the gravity of the situation in Zephaniah's day and, as we will see, the amazing scope of redemption as it is sketched in Zephaniah 3. For now, we can observe several important points about the judgment that the prophet announces in the light of God's beautiful, flawless, and pure creation before human sin.

What first catches the attention of the reader in Zephaniah 1:2 is the apparently unlimited scope of God's punishment. He affirms that He will "utterly consume everything" from the face of the earth. To emphasize the extent of this destructive event, verse 3 lists the primary human and animal subjects of creation in reverse order, working back through Genesis 1: "man and beast" (day 6) and "the birds of the heavens, the fish of the sea" (day 5). Not even the flood that follows later in Genesis included the fish and the birds.

Yet God's judgment, even if it seems to sweep away all before it, is not indiscriminate, careless, or unjust, for it focuses on "the wicked" (Zeph. 1:3). Zephaniah's language is meant to strike fear into all insofar as every human being is potentially threatened by this judgment. Further, the interrelationship between human beings and the world in which they live means that the rest of the created order cannot escape unscathed from such divine punishment. (Second Peter 3:10 says that "the earth and the works that are in it will be burned up.") Even now, the whole creation "groans" under the "futility" that God's curse on sin and various aspects of fallen human existence (Genesis 3) have brought on the world (Rom. 8:19–22).

The judgment portrayed in Zephaniah 1:2–3, 14–18 is the framework in which the more limited but still frightful judgment of Judah is to be understood (vv. 4–13). Unlike verses 4–13, where numerous terms refer to Jerusalem, its rulers, and various individuals and groups within the nation of Judah, the framework around the central section lacks any terms that limit this flood-like judgment. In fact, the text stresses the contrary. The

term "man/men" (*'adam*; 1:3, 17) is the broadest possible reference to human beings, and especially in light of Zephaniah 2,
it is impossible to limit all "the land" (or "earth," ESV, twice in
1:18) to Judah. There are still more echoes of the creation of
humanity in verse 17, with "blood" (see Gen. 9:6) expressing the
radically fatal effects of God's wrath against sin and being compared to the "dust" to which sinful humanity's body returns after
death (see Gen. 2:7; 3:19).

God's word through Zephaniah, addressed first to Judah but
ultimately to the whole world, is rooted in His supremely important role as Creator and Judge of every human being. His "very
good" creation and the divine holiness that it faintly reflected,
above all in Adam and Eve, mean that God's very being is absolutely incompatible with sin in any form. His justice, moreover,
demands that sin be punished in a way that captures the great
significance of human actions as God's image-bearers and especially His inexpressible purity and perfection. Much like Adam
and Eve's sin broke their harmonious relationship of fellowship
and life with God, Zephaniah 1:2–3, 14–18 announces that a
punishment greater than the flood in Noah's day is coming on
all who persist in their attempt to live in God's world as God's
image-bearers, but without honoring, fearing, or obeying Him.

Sin and Judgment Today

Because no one in a state of rebellion against God will survive
this judgment, Zephaniah's message is applicable to everyone, no
less today than in the late seventh century BC. This biblical foundation for understanding ourselves, the world around us, and the
fact that God "has appointed a day on which He will judge the
world" (Acts 17:31) runs completely contrary to the narratives

that sinful human beings fabricate for themselves and put their trust in. While there are innumerable forms in which such a worldview can express itself, the basic elements are rejections of those at the center of Zephaniah's reprise of the flood: the only living God— sovereign, holy, and just—has created humanity in His image and with the intention that they glorify Him by obedient service offered in love, ruling the created order in such a way that creation itself is "a response of praise to its maker."[2] Fallen humanity, from the first couple until today, has chosen to go their own way, which involves first the decision to determine for themselves what is true, good, and necessary. This rebellion inevitably works itself out in all spheres of life and in every aspect of human existence. Our will is deformed, our mind is unable to grasp truth, our heart is unwilling to give up its autonomy. Despite God's patience, this situation can only end in the definitive punishment of sinful human beings by the just, holy, and omnipotent God who created them and whose law condemns them.

It is this diagnosis of humanity that underlies Zephaniah's message of judgment (and salvation, as we will see) and that motivates the church's faithful preaching of the gospel to the world at large, without compromise and with love and humility. We must not forget that we, too, were "disobedient, deceived," and enslaved to innumerable sins (Titus 3:3). In a beautiful paradox, salvation from this coming judgment is possible only because the God whom Zephaniah presents here in the role of Judge is also the only Savior of those threatened by that judgment (Zeph. 1:4–5). Although there is no messianic figure in Zephaniah, the themes of creation, sin, and death, as worked

---

2. Colin Gunton, *The Triune Creator: A Historical and Systematic Study* (Grand Rapids: Eerdmans, 1998), 12.

out in the life of the first Adam and his posterity, are marvelously taken up in the second Adam, whose substitutionary death exhausts divine wrath against sin and whose obedience merits life. In Jesus Christ, both benefits are graciously shared with those who turn from their sin and trust in Him for deliverance.

Questions for Reflection

1. In what ways does the doctrine of creation help explain the natural human predicament as being under condemnation?

2. What are some current worldviews or cultural trends that reject key elements of biblical teaching concerning what human beings are, to whom they are accountable, and the ability of humanity to find its own meaning and security apart from God?

3. How might Christians err in the same way?

4. How should Zephaniah's stark description of sin's horrific consequences fuel our desire to follow God more fully?

Resources

Gunton, Colin. *The Triune Creator: A Historical and Systematic Study*. Grand Rapids: Eerdmans, 1998. 246 pp. A demanding but rewarding theology of creation that highlights the Trinitarian nature of creation and its relation to redemption.

CHAPTER 9

Sin and Its Outcomes,
with a Call to Repent

Zephaniah 1:4–13; 2:1–3

Although the judgment announced in Zephaniah 1:2–3, 14–18 potentially includes all human beings, it is still surprising—and was surely shocking to much of Zephaniah's original audience (v. 12)—to see that God first focuses His condemnation on His people in Judah. Still more unexpected is the center of this focus, the city of Jerusalem, where His temple stood and where descendants of David reigned as vice-regents on His throne (1 Chron. 28:5). While some of this can be attributed to Jerusalem representing the rest of Judah (hence, "Judah…Jerusalem" [Zeph. 1:4]), Zephaniah's critiques are often directed against royalty and other leaders in Judah (1:4, 8).

This shows that even those who were responsible for leading God's people with God-given authority were in large part unfaithful in their roles. In what follows, we will explore not simply what sins were practiced and thus fell under prophetic condemnation, but *why* these sins were practiced. What advantages did those who practiced them expect to gain from acting as they did? What beliefs had they embraced or rejected to arrive at that point? How had sin deceived them (Heb. 3:13)? Answers to these questions will help us see how sin works, diagnose it in our own lives, and pursue deliverance from sin in repentance and in union with Christ in His death and resurrection.

Religion as a Self-Serving Tool

All corrupt religious practice, regardless of the deity or ideal to which it is directed, is intended to advance the interests and serve the desires of the worshiper. As Zephaniah shows, even those raised in a monotheistic, theocratic society in which God's prophets were generally free to speak against people and king alike are hardly immune to such corruptions of religious teaching and practice. The prophet's first critique starts with perhaps the most radical form of such deformation, meaning the outright rejection of Yahweh in favor of the god Baal. Baal was worshiped in various ways across much of the ancient Levant (eastern Mediterranean region) and was generally associated with the concept of fertility, whether human, agricultural, or animal, as well as the afterlife. He was also believed to occasionally act as defender of those who worshiped him, as texts from the Syrian city of Ugarit show.[1] His worshipers would thus pray to him for children (see, for example, the Kirta epic) or for dew and rain so that their crops would grow; for the well-being of dead ancestors; and for protection when at sea or under attack.[2]

This means that Judean worshipers of Baal, despite what they knew from the Old Testament Scriptures that they would have heard read, taught, or discussed, discounted Scripture's consistent affirmation of God's sovereignty, goodness, and omnipotence in favor of belief in Baal. This was nothing other than the people's attempt to take control of their lives regardless

---

1. Daniel C. Timmer, "Ugaritic Ritual in Epic, Cult, and the Everyday: Paradigms for the Interpenetration of History and Religion in Second-Millennium Canaanite Culture," *Revue d'Études des Civilisations Anciennes du Proche-Orient* 14 (2008–2009): 17–26.

2. Wolfgang Herrmann, "Baal," in *Dictionary of Deities and Demons*, ed. K. van der Toorn, B. Becking, and P. van der Horst, 2nd ed. (Leiden: Brill, 1999), 132–39.

of what God might do (see Zeph. 1:12). In these people's minds, worshiping Baal by prayer, sacrifices, and other actions was more likely to bring them what they desired than was faithful, obedient life in fellowship with Yahweh. Not being omnipotent or sovereign, Baal was also more open to manipulation and coercion than was the God of Israel. If God's prophets announced judgments that threatened the agricultural produce that these Judeans needed to survive, they clearly believed that such threats could be countered by invoking Baal. Yet Baal was not the winner in this exchange—the worshiper gave to get, and Baal served as the means to that end. Both "idolatrous priests" and ordinary priests were involved in this blatant idolatry (v. 4).

Other Judeans pursued the same project of self-determination, or autonomy, by serving celestial deities, often believed to be able to predict or reveal the future through various forms of divination (see 2 Kings 23:4–5). Still others attempted to blend worship of Yahweh with worship of Milcom (Zeph. 1:5), a reference to the highest Ammonite deity. This may have been due to the impression that Ammon's increasing prowess in the seventh century was proof of this deity's power, providing a way for these Judeans to hedge their bets and protect themselves in case God failed to protect them.[3]

Similar trust in foreign powers is at issue with the rather puzzling reference to the clothing worn by the king's sons and others (Zeph. 1:8). These articles of clothing are condemned not for their foreign origin but for their religious and political significance as indications that the Judean elite looked to other nations

---

3. Joel S. Burnett, "Transjordan: The Ammonites, Moabites, and Edomites," in *The World around the Old Testament: The People and Places of the Ancient Near East*, ed. B. T. Arnold and B. A. Strawn (Grand Rapids: Baker Academic, 2016), 319, 346.

for security. Even the Judean royal court, ruled by a descendant of David to whom God had pledged His care and protection (2 Samuel 7; Psalm 2), lacked the kind of commitment to God and trust in Him that would provide stability even when the nation was in difficulty.

With leaders like these, it is hardly surprising that Judean society had wandered far from God and His law. Superstition, as exhibited in the practice of leaping over the threshold of a door under which cult statues of one or more deities were buried, demonstrated the belief that such deities could protect that location from demons or the like. "Violence and deceit" were practiced by the servants of the powerful (Zeph. 1:9), whose houses were filled with goods acquired at the expense of the weaker and more vulnerable members of society whom they should have protected (Ex. 22:22; Deut. 10:18–19). Whether those who "turned back from following the LORD" (Zeph. 1:6) and totally ignored Him also practiced these and other evils, the root sin in all these cases is almost identical to that of Adam and Eve: acting on the mistaken belief that a person can do better without God and His guidance and blessing than with Him. All sin is thus, at its root, a violation of the first commandment.

Sin and Its Fitting Punishment

But how wrong these Judeans were! Their sins will be met with suitable punishment, and that in two senses. First, as a violation of God's will, sins are punishable as such. But sin's deceitful character means that it never brings to the sinner what it promises or promotes. Indeed, it usually brings the opposite. God's outstretched hand and His promise to "cut off" sinners in

Zephaniah 1:4 makes clear that sin will be punished by death, and this idea is presented in a shocking way in verse 7:

> Be silent in the presence of the Lord GOD;
> For the day of the LORD is at hand,
> For the LORD has prepared a sacrifice;
> He has invited His guests.

Here God warns that the day of the Lord is near and describes it as a feast. But this feast is not one in which the guests celebrate. On the contrary, they are consecrated (or "invited") in the same way that the sacrifice is set aside for death! As an immediate response to those who put their trust mostly or wholly in other gods (vv. 4–6), this death threat is suitable not merely as a punishment for sin in general, but especially as the inevitable consequence of seeking meaning, stability, and life apart from God.

God's intervention punishes in a similar way the economic activity of those who bought and sold unjustly, as their business ventures come to nothing (Zeph. 1:11). Most ironically, Yahweh's judgment will fall on those who believed that He was inactive, doing neither good nor evil (v. 12). The punishment for that unbelief is inevitably proof that God is active, and He imposes the punishments for covenant infidelity laid out in Deuteronomy 28. Those who have amassed wealth unjustly will lose it, and the imminent exile of Judah will see the people lose their houses and their land as well. Their inability to drink the wine that their vineyards produce, the outcome of a futility curse, perfectly illustrates the tenor of the punishments Zephaniah lists in chapter 1. Whatever people think to gain in pursing something or someone other than God as uppermost they inevitably lose, along with their life and soul (unless there is repentance).

A Call to Repent

Despite the chapter division after Zephaniah 1:18, the call to seek the Lord in 2:1–3 should be considered as a guide for how Zephaniah's audience and later readers ought to respond to the divine accusations and condemnations announced in chapter 1. The very presence of a call to repent, along with the possibility (somewhat qualified) of deliverance from the judgments looming over Judah, is noteworthy considering the apparently absolute nature of Zephaniah's condemnations of all humanity in 1:2–3, 14–18. As we have seen, however, God's justice is not careless or blunt, and the prophet has consistently connected divine judgment with those guilty of particular sins or entirely committed to a sinful lifestyle (for example, "the wicked"; 1:3).

This call to repentance proposes a remedy diametrically opposed to the sin it targets: "Seek the LORD" and "Seek righteousness, seek humility" (2:3). Rather than seeking other gods or simply trying to live in complete independence, Zephaniah calls his audience to a radical reorientation of their hearts and lives. To seek the Lord in the face of His imminent punishment of Judah is to take Him at His word, to reckon Him truthful and able to impose such a punishment (contrast 1:12). It is at the same time to jettison any dream of escaping His justice and to discount one's own view of right and wrong in favor of His. It is, finally, for the people to recognize in all humility that repentance may not deliver them from sin's immediate, temporal consequences. It is for this reason that this call to repentance ends with "It may be that you will be hidden in the day of the LORD's anger" (2:3). This is not God's refusal to forgive and pardon those who turn to Him, but rather the affirmation that because whatever judgment comes on Judah will affect all Judeans, there is no guarantee that the penitent will escape invasion, exile, or even a violent death at the hands of Judah's enemies.

The Judeans who repent as directed by Zephaniah and in light of this warning of coming divine punishment of Judah change radically. While the "meek of the earth" (2:3) are mentioned specifically, the call is issued to the entire nation (v. 1). Whether the meek grow in humility and obedience or formerly idolatrous Judeans abandon their false god(s) and submit to Yahweh from the heart, a radically different group (called "the remnant" in 2:7, 9) emerges within Judah. It is this radical change that Zephaniah's message, made effective by God's power, should bring about in its hearers then and now.

If even the humble of the land need to seek the Lord, how much more do we? Zephaniah excludes from the outset any idea of qualifying for or meriting God's grace. Furthermore, whatever level of sanctification and holiness a believer has achieved to date, this prophetic warning is still relevant considering the ongoing fulfillment of the day of the Lord and its final stage in the day of Christ's return. It calls believers to sanctify and prepare themselves for that great day (1 Thess. 5:1–11). Those who fail to do so risk finding themselves saved, yes, but "as through fire" (1 Cor. 3:15). In view of sin's deceitful nature on the one hand and God's unmeasurable goodness on the other hand, what reason can we give to avoid the relentless pursuit of repentance, fellowship with God through His Son and by His Spirit, and a life of joyful, grateful obedience that witnesses by word and deed to His greatness and glory?

Questions for Reflection

1. Think of some sins with which you continue to struggle and try to identify ways in which that process involves your being deceived. What truths should you meditate on and pray over to correct those patterns of thinking?

2. In what ways might some of your religious beliefs or practices (right or wrong in themselves) be self-serving, at least in part? Examples might include undervaluing God's holiness, taking pride in your perceived doctrinal correctness, or mentioning others' faults in ways that damage their reputation while enhancing yours.

3. The first of Martin Luther's Ninety-Five Theses reads thus: "When our Lord and Master Jesus Christ said 'Repent,' he willed the entire life of believers to be one of repentance."[4] How does this emphasis connect with Paul's exhortations to put off one's old nature and to put on the new, or the New Testament pattern of dying and rising with Christ? See Romans 6:4; Heidelberg Catechism 43, 45; Westminster Confession of Faith 13; Westminster Larger Catechism 75–76.

Resources

Plantinga, Cornelius Jr. *Not the Way It's Supposed to Be: A Breviary of Sin*. Grand Rapids: Eerdmans, 1995. 216 pp. An excellent, concise, and insightful exploration of sin.

---

4. *Martin Luther's Basic Theological Writings*, ed. Timothy F. Lull, 2nd ed. (Minneapolis: Fortress, 2005), 41.

CHAPTER 10

The Judgment or Salvation
of the Nations

Zephaniah 2:4–15

Much as Zephaniah 1 focused on the global condemnation of sin (vv. 2–3, 14–18) and on Judah (vv. 4–13), most of chapter 2 brings that general condemnation to bear on non-Israelites. Non-Israelites, especially in the role of the nations, often manifest opposition to or at least nonchalance before God's actions on behalf of His people. This dynamic is evident as early as God's promise to bless "all the families of the earth" through Abraham and his descendants and to curse the one "who curses" Abraham's line (Gen. 12:3). Despite the often-adversarial relationships between Israel or Judah and the non-Israelite nations, the Old Testament consistently affirms but also develops this two-sided reality.

The Psalms in particular emphasize both aspects of Israel's role in the world, affirming that the nations should recognize God's rule through His anointed king or face His wrath (e.g., Pss. 2; 22:27) and calling the nations, directly or indirectly, to know God and exult in Him (Pss. 47:1; 49:1; 67:3, 5; 72:11, 17; 86:9; 96:3; 102:15; 117:1). Zephaniah 2 does the same, although the emphasis falls on the negative side of this relationship because of the ways that many of the surrounding nations have treated God's people in the recent past. In the middle of this section, however, verse 11 connects the book's clearest statement so far of salvation to non-Israelites.

Yahweh against Some of the Nations

The strong emphasis of Zephaniah 2 on the divine judgment that will come on the nations because of their mistreatment of God's people and the pride that motivates such actions reflects the typical role of non-Israelite nations in the life of Israel from the beginning of the nation's history. Apart from the beneficent pharaoh of Joseph's day and a few more exceptions, such as Rahab and the queen of Sheba, the peoples around Israel pursued their own designs, often at Israel's expense. The Philistines in the time of Saul and David, the Syrians now and again, and especially the Assyrian Empire and the Babylonian Empire after it, interacted with Israel and Judah with the goal of securing their own destinies, defending themselves against perceived threats, taking necessary natural resources by force, capturing foreigners to use as slaves, and (in the case of Assyria and Babylon) pursuing the realization of an imperial ideology that they thought entitled them to subdue the world around them as proof of their gods' superior power.

Actions like these, and especially the attitudes and worldviews that drive them, are at the heart of Yahweh's and Zephaniah's critiques of the Philistines (Zeph. 2:4–7), Moab and Ammon (vv. 8–10), Ethiopia (or Cush in some Bible translations; v. 12), and Assyria (vv. 13–15). The first two sections, dealing with the Philistines and Moab and Ammon, are notable for including the benefit that will come to the faithful Judean remnant because of God's punishment of their and His enemies. Philistine territory will become pastures for the livestock of "the

remnant of the house of Judah" (vv. 6–7) as part of God's larger
work of restoration in which He brings an end to the punishment prophesied in chapter 1. Similarly, Moabite and Ammonite
goods will be plundered and taken by those whom they had pre-
viously antagonized (v. 9), and Nineveh will be so completely
destroyed that only wild animals will inhabit it (v. 14).

In all but the first case, God makes clear why His judgment
will come on these nations. In the case of Moab and Ammon,
their "reproach" for and dismissive attitude toward Judah, whom
God expressly identifies as "My people" (v. 8), are the cause. This
point is made again in verse 10, where these actions are tied to
the root cause of pride that leads them to mistreat "the people
of the LORD of hosts." In mistreating Judah, Moab and Ammon
have slighted the God who identifies Himself with His people,
who promises to protect them, and who dwells among them. It is
important to note that God's attitude toward non-Israelites takes
no account of their ethnicity or race and is determined solely by
their response to Him (and, by association, to His people).

The link between a person's fate and his or her view of self
and of God is still clearer in the case of the much more powerful Assyrian Empire, whose punishment is explained in verse 15.
Almost to the end of its existence at the close of the seventh century BC, Assyria celebrated itself and its gods, proclaiming its
and their undeniable superiority. The self-congratulatory capital
city of Nineveh, supremely confident in the empire's military
power and diplomatic apparatus, is personified as a queen who
asserts her incomparability and grandeur, saying "in her heart, 'I
am it, and there is none besides me'" (v. 15). Indeed, Assyria's
massive pride echoes God's own statements of His incomparability in Isaiah (45:6; 46:9). Such hubris cannot go unpunished,

and God commits to bringing this massive empire down, something that came to pass during or immediately after Zephaniah's ministry. In summary, God's punishment of the nations in this chapter deconstructs their proud claims to significance or even world dominion, ensures the survival of the remnant of His peoples, and demonstrates His supremacy over all who would supplant Him or oppose His purposes.

Yahweh for Some among the Nations

As Genesis 12 makes clear, God's purposes for the nations are not limited to judgment. This wonderful truth is presented with amazing clarity in Zephaniah 2:11. Rather than mentioning a particular nation, Zephaniah mentions the "shores" that are at the farthest remove from Israel—over the horizon, so to speak. Even though God's work among His own people is currently at a low ebb due to their sin, this will not thwart His promise to bring blessing far and wide through them. This verse emphasizes God's sovereign work as the one who makes Himself known to non-Israelites. The spiritual nature of this work is evident from Zephaniah's description of it. God will "reduce to nothing all the gods of the earth," showing that they have nothing in common with Him and that He alone deserves to be revered and worshiped. In the face of His power and holiness, all other so-called gods are weak and short-lived.

This demonstration of the Lord's unique supremacy as Creator, Judge, and Savior leads to a very surprising outcome, particularly in the context of Zephaniah 2. Rather than opposing God or seeking to avoid Him, these non-Israelites will worship or bow down to Him in recognition of His unique deity and in demonstration of their submission to Him. This puts them in the same category as the faithful Judean remnant that will "seek the LORD" in verse 3 but contrasts them with the Judeans who worship other gods in chapter 1. Of course, it also distinguishes them from the other non-Israelites in chapter 2, who pursued their own purposes in proud disdain for Yahweh and His people. Although a detailed description of God's joy over His people appears only later in Zephaniah, it is safe to assume here that these non-Israelites celebrate His grace to them once they are delivered from the vain worship of their now-defunct deities. As shown by the focus on the heart attitudes of the non-Israelites in this chapter, their well-being is inseparable from their religious conversion.

Questions for Reflection

1. Given the priority of Israel as the initial recipients of God's covenant and grace, how should Gentiles view their grafting into them (see Rom. 11:9–24)?

2. How should we pray for the Jewish people?

3. What priorities and responsibilities should Christians and Christian churches have with respect to missions, whether foreign or domestic? Where does evangelism fit into the Christian life?

4. Why do you think pride figures so largely in God's condemnation of foreign nations in chapter 2 and of Judah in chapter 3? To what degree does pride play a role in the sins you see in your life? How can we fight against our pride?

Note the ironic boasting that Paul associates with those who find their salvation in Christ crucified (Gal. 6:14).

Resources

Murray, Iain H. *The Puritan Hope: Revival and the Interpretation of Prophecy*. Edinburgh: Banner of Truth, 1971. 361 pp. An edifying exposition of the place of God's old covenant people in the New Testament era.

Piper, John. *Let the Nations Be Glad! The Supremacy of God in Missions*. 3rd ed. Grand Rapids: Baker Academic, 2010. 288 pp. A God-centered, practical explanation of Christian mission.

CHAPTER 11

Sin, Judgment—and Salvation
Zephaniah 3

So far, the book of Zephaniah has presented almost without exception the problem of human sin and the divine judgment that will inevitably come on unrepentant sinners. The only glimpses of hope within its message to this point are the call to repent (2:1–3), the abrupt appearance of Judah's remnant (vv. 7, 9), and the prediction that some non-Israelites will worship God (v. 11).

Chapter 3 begins in a way that reinforces, one last time, the immensity of the problem of sin before the book's final section presents in unprecedented depth and scope God's gracious work of salvation for His people and for non-Israelites. This strategy of surprise is surely intended to elicit faith and repentance in the reader who is aware of his or her sin. No less surprisingly, the book's final section also reveals to the reader God's delight in the sinners whom He saves. This, perhaps even more than the threat of judgment, exerts a powerful pull on the reader, who now understands the glory of God's love as well as the wonderfully transforming power of His grace.

The Rebellious City

Because the identity of the city that is the subject of Zephaniah 3:1–7 is not made clear right away, the reader might assume that Nineveh, discussed in 2:13–15, is still in view. It would be reasonable to think so. As we saw in our discussion of Nahum, Nineveh was very closely associated with the violence and oppression that were at the heart of the empire. Yet readers soon learn of this city that Yahweh is "her God" (3:2), something that could never be said of Nineveh and could be said only of Jerusalem. This possible confusion highlights the main point of the section. Jerusalem, although the capital city of Judah and closely associated with the God of Israel whose presence was there (v. 5), has more in common with Nineveh than with her God!

When read along with 2:1–3, this section implies that the call to repent was not heeded by most of Zephaniah's audience. The focus here is on Judah's leaders, called to serve God by leading and protecting His people (the king), teaching the law and preserving the purity of the sacrificial system (the priests), transmitting Yahweh's word to His people (the prophets), and establishing justice (the judges). But the city and its leaders are both terribly far from these ideals. The city is disobedient and oppressive, and the same is true of her leaders. Jerusalem's leaders and judges are compared to lions and wolves who consume their fellow citizens (especially their material wealth) as a beast of prey consumes its victims (3:3). The false prophets recklessly speak of their own accord and use their message to corrupt and mislead the people they claim to serve.[1] For their part, the priests act in direct contradiction to their God-given vocation to distinguish between the holy and the common (Lev. 10:10) and to teach the law to the people (2 Chron. 17:7–9). In a word, many of the leaders of Judah have not only chosen not to follow God themselves but are using their office and authority to lead

---

1. J. J. M. Roberts, *Nahum, Habakkuk, Zephaniah: A Commentary*, Old Testament Library (Louisville, Ky.: Westminster/John Knox, 1991), 213.

the people away from Him or to abuse and oppress them. Put more pointedly, the leaders act like non-Israelite nations bent on doing harm to God's people and using them for their own purposes. And all this takes place despite God's supernatural presence residing in the temple at the heart of this very same city (Zeph. 3:5)!

To this dire diagnosis God adds one more element. As a sort of object lesson, He reminds His people that the defeats and invasions they have witnessed in the nations around them, especially as Assyria tightened its control on the Levant, were meant to show to Judah the consequences of living in violation of God's will (v. 6). But Judah has not paid attention—in fact, they have become worse, doubling down on their commitment to advance themselves in the face of God's claims over them!

Judgment—and Salvation!

It is therefore no surprise that God's patience with His people has come to an end (Zeph. 3:8). As is often the case in Zephaniah, the text seems to rule out any possibility of deliverance. God Himself will seize His prey, which seems to include all nations and peoples. His anger against sin in Judah and among the nations is now red hot and threatens to consume them entirely. And yet what follows in verses 9–20 shows that God establishes justice in two ways. Punitively, He brings down the just punishment of sin on those who persist in their disobedience, rebellion, and autonomy, something we have seen throughout the book. But God also manifests His righteousness by delivering from sin and its consequences those whom He chooses—and delights—to save. This salvation is the exclusive focus of verses 9–20, which explain and meditate on God's purifying, renewing, and saving work in His people, both Jew and Gentile.

Speaking through Zephaniah, God first presents another perspective on His transforming grace at work in the hearts of non-Israelites (3:9) before turning to Judah (v. 10). The description of God's saving work among the peoples is puzzling at first glance:

> For then I will restore to the peoples a pure language,
> That they all may call on the name of the LORD,
> To serve Him with one accord. (v. 9)

How can changed speech lead to worship of Yahweh and corporate obedience to Him? This metaphor involves no change of language on the level of Pentecost but rather on the level of the heart, the contents of which the mouth expresses (Prov. 15:28; Matt. 15:18). The purification of Isaiah's lips in Isaiah 6 captures this process perfectly. There the prophet bemoans his "unclean lips" (v. 5) in the blinding light of the Lord's holiness, which has shaken the temple and overwhelms even the seraphim in His presence (vv. 1–4). The lips thus symbolize the expression of what is in the heart, and as a sinful human being, Isaiah recognizes his urgent need for purification lest God's holiness consume him. The solution to Isaiah's dilemma bears this out. In Isaiah's vision, a coal from the altar of burnt offering is touched to his lips, and on that basis God's messenger announces that his "iniquity is taken away" and his "sin purged" (v. 7).

We can conclude on this basis that Zephaniah 3:9 announces a radical transformation among those nations who had formerly oppressed God's people, arrogantly scorned His authority, and pursued their own designs for their own glory. In a way that draws attention to God's sovereignty in the work of salvation, He states that He will change the hearts of these non-Israelites in the most profound way possible. Rather than scorning His claims to deity and trusting in other gods, they now look to Him alone for pardon, deliverance, and blessing. Rather than attacking one another in a power-hungry riot of military and political conflicts, the nations are united in their service to Yahweh, ordering every aspect of their persons, lives, and activity in view of who He is.

The same radical work of purification and transformation will renew God's chosen people. The theme of renewal is introduced with the idea of their return from exile far away (beyond Ethiopia, or Cush), culminating in their worship of Him at the temple (v. 10). This change is described in more detail here than anywhere else in the book. First, God promises to remove the shame associated with their sins against Him. Second, restored Israel/Judah will be without "those who rejoice in…pride" (v. 11) and arrogant individuals who trusted in their own strength and made their plans and desires uppermost.

In positive terms, this renewed people of God will be characterized above all by meekness and humility, expressed in the awareness of their total dependence on God (cf. "poor in spirit" in Matt. 5:3 and the parallel "poor" in Luke 6:20). This dependence makes them "trust in" ("seek refuge in," ESV) the name of the Lord (Zeph. 3:12). Continuing the focus on the mouth as what expresses the contents and desires of the heart, God states that His renewed people will do no unrighteousness "and speak no lies, nor shall a deceitful tongue be found in their mouth" (v. 13).

These statements depict more than a sanctified life—they are evidence of a heart purified of *all* sin, not only justified but fully sanctified and perfected. It is for this reason that they can graze and "lie down" (v. 13), with no fear of an enemy. Not only have their external enemies been removed, but sin as their longtime internal enemy no longer exists. This passage depicts the full and final stage of salvation for God's people, whom He shepherds forever in green pastures without sin, danger, or interruption.

This is still clearer in the call for the "daughter of Zion" to shout her praise to God (vv. 14–15).

> "Sing, O daughter of Zion!
> Shout, O Israel!
> Be glad and rejoice with all your heart, O daughter
>   of Jerusalem!
> The LORD has taken away your judgments,
> He has cast out your enemy.
> The King of Israel, the LORD, is in your midst;
> You shall see disaster no more."

Wholehearted, fervent praise is the only possible response to divine salvation that removes both God's just condemnation of His people and their internal and external enemies (v. 15). Because God is present with them in the fullest sense of the phrase, His worshipers are subject neither to fear nor to weakness but are aware of their perfect security in His presence and their readiness to fulfill His will perfectly.

This exceptional depiction of the experience of those who are perfected and glorified is matched only by Zephaniah's description of this same relationship from God's side. The prophet directs his audience's attention to Yahweh's superlative presence with them and power exercised for their deliverance before he reveals God's inexpressible love for His people in unparalleled terms. The omnipotent Creator who is eternally self-sufficient and satisfied in His Trinitarian existence

will rejoice over you with gladness,
He will quiet you with His love,
He will rejoice over you with singing. (3:17)

God's love, stronger than their sin and all other opposition to His saving purposes for them, will quiet and satisfy them. And amid this perfect stillness and wholeness of soul, God Himself fills their ears with His celebration of them as His people, adopted children, and covenant partners (Isa. 65:17–19).

This all-too-brief glance at the final stage of God's work of redemption, with His perfected people living and worshiping in His presence and God Himself singing over them, brings the book of Zephaniah full circle. From the initial backdrop of a sinless but fallible creation, God has pursued His restorative and redemptive purposes, punishing sin and maintaining His justice while also making possible deliverance from that punishment. Zephaniah has done his utmost to convince his fellow Judeans that sin in all its forms inevitably leads to death, while only God can bring about the spiritual renewal that leads to repentance, faith, and fidelity to Him. Despite its often-dark colors, the message of Zephaniah is thus shot through with rays of hope that have their origin in God's gracious and compassionate character, which weds forgiveness and justice (Ex. 34:6–7), righteousness and peace (Ps. 85:10).

Questions for Reflection

1. How do the critiques of Judah's leaders in Zephaniah 3:1–4 help explain Peter's call in 1 Peter 5:1–4 for elders and pastors (shepherds) to exercise oversight as ready servants of God who use their authority to protect those under their care without being domineering? What attitudes should church members have toward those who shepherd them as Peter urges?

2. The truth that God's work renews the hearts of His people rather than simply changes some external behaviors is wonderfully encouraging for those who realize how deeply rooted their remaining sin is. Since the new creation that much of Zephaniah 3 describes is fully realized in Christ and has begun in believers, how can our fellowship with Him draw more deeply on His power, grace, and love as we struggle in the already–not yet of the Christian life?

3. Meditate on God's love for you in Jesus Christ. How and why have you not given this amazing reality the attention and meditation that it should receive? How can you remedy this with God's help?

Resources

Carson, D. A. *The Difficult Doctrine of the Love of God.* Wheaton, Ill.: Crossway, 1999. 96 pp. A careful and edifying discussion of the rich biblical presentation of God's love.

Morgan, Christopher W., ed. *The Love of God*. Theology in Community. Wheaton, Ill.: Crossway, 2016. 256 pp. A broad and rich treatment of God's love from a variety of perspectives.

Ortlund, Dane. *Gentle and Lowly: The Heart of Christ for Sinners and Sufferers*. Wheaton, Ill.: Crossway, 2020. 224 pp. A very pastoral, heart-searching meditation on Christ and His marvelous sufficiency for needs of all kinds.

Williams, Gary. *His Love Endures Forever: Meditations on the Immeasurable Love of God*. Wheaton, Ill.: Crossway, 2016. 223 pp. A theologically robust series of extended meditations on God's love and its role in the Christian life.